LIVING WITH
BORROWED DUST

Also by James Hollis

LIVING WITH BORROWED DUST

Reflections on Life, Love, and Other Grievances

JAMES HOLLIS, PhD

sounds true
BOULDER, COLORADO

Sounds True
Boulder, CO

Published 2025

Cover design by Jennifer Miles
Book and jacket design by Meredith Jarrett

Printed in Canada

BK07142

Library of Congress Cataloging-in-Publication Data

Names: Hollis, James, 1940- author.
Title: Living with borrowed dust : reflections on life, love, and other
    grievances / James Hollis, Ph.D.
Description: Boulder, CO : Sounds True, 2025. | Includes bibliographical
    references.
Identifiers: LCCN 2024022374 (print) | LCCN 2024022375 (ebook) |
    ISBN 9781649633484 (trade paperback) | ISBN 9781649633491
    (ebook)
Subjects: LCSH: Jungian psychology. | Happiness. | Hollis,
    James, 1940-
Classification: LCC BF173 .H725 2025 (print) |
    LCC BF173 (ebook) | DDC 150.19/54--dc23/
    eng/20241025
LC record available at https://lccn.loc.gov/2024022374
LC ebook record available at
    https://lccn.loc.gov/2024022375

FSC
www.fsc.org
MIX
Paper | Supporting
responsible forestry
FSC® C016245

*This book is for Jill, the love
of my life, and our children:
Taryn and Tim, Jonah and Seah.*

*With thanks also to Liz Harrison
and Lyric Dodson, Angela Wix, and
Anastasia Pellouchoud of Sounds True
for their part in making this book happen.*

I only borrowed this dust.

—Stanley Kunitz

The mind that is not baffled is not employed. The impeded stream is the one that sings.

—Wendell Berry

Every light, every fire, comes to an end, and there would be utter darkness, but there is still left the light of the self, which is the supreme light.

—C. G. Jung

The experience of Self brings a feeling of standing on solid ground inside oneself, on a patch of eternity, which even physical death cannot touch.

—Marie-Louise von Franz

Character—the willingness to accept responsibility for one's own life—is the source from which self-respect springs.

—Joan Didion

Contents

FOREWORD

I have been reading James Hollis's writings and listening to his podcasts for many years. He never ceases to amaze, delight, and instruct me in his books and talks. His insights into the human condition are deeply instructive, delivered with a light hand and a sense of humor. He is, first and foremost, a doctor of the soul.

The trilogy of disciplines he employs in his work are depth psychology, mythology, and poetry. As one whose field is literary studies and depth psychology, I find a kindred spirit in Hollis's insights into our frail, uncertain, and suffering lives, whose search for meaning is one of the hallmarks of Hollis's vision of being human. His own training, as many of you know, was in literary studies. Then he heard and responded to the call to become a Jungian analyst. He never lost his first love's richness and continues to be infused with poetry's wisdom tradition.

One of many areas that he continues to cultivate here is that the human species is an energy-conducting, absorbing, and transferring body, in the spirit of Pierre Teilhard de Chardin and Joseph Campbell. He shares with the latter the idea that courage is needed for one's life journey—to enter the woods where it is thickest and where no path reveals itself. Then, one is on one's own authentic pilgrimage. Often this quest is prompted by questions Hollis encourages all of us to ask in service to the soul's search for meaning: "What are you in service of?" "What are you called to serve?" Not seriously contemplating such prompts is to invite a life of habitual thinking and behaving that keeps one safely cocooned in certainty and on the outer rim of psychic and spiritual growth.

Narrative is also at the heart of Hollis's thinking about the soul's meaningful life—the story we tell ourselves in our quest for meaning or as armor against such an undertaking. His focus on the nature of stories, the one we know and the deeper story that knows us, he suggests, encourages a double discovery of what our life means. Another rhetorical strategy in *Living with Borrowed Dust* is the genius of one-liners, pithy insights into the human condition, like the following: "Nothing is more evanescent than a need satisfied." These are meant for us to ponder, to take us more deeply into our life experience, to open us to new ways of thinking about our comfortable storyline, and perhaps to take the pen of revision to it not once but often.

I continue to be drawn to Hollis's insight that Jung himself tapped: the mythopoetic nature of the human psyche as well as Jung's development of "active imagination" that are described elegantly in this volume as ways to create conversations between conscious and unconscious, between ego and self. So this volume serves as a handbook of sorts. One does not simply read it; one is encouraged to move the insights into a praxis, to feel their value in existence.

There is also, present throughout the book, the feel of a memoir, not simply a reminiscence on his life and work but more a revision of it in relation to his and his wife, Jill's, new life in assisted living and the process of aging. Remembrance, yes, but more: an imaginal recollection that is another opportunity to see himself through the prism of a long and challenging history. From this vantage point, he reminds us of one of his favorite axioms: "It's all not about what it's about."

Authenticity is another watchword in Hollis's lexicon that speaks of resilience and rediscovery, of recovering and reshaping parts of each of us that may have been lost in the matrix of modernity, with its addiction to the horizontal at the expense of life's deepening, where the soul is fed and renewed. That sense of authenticity also grows from an attitude that Hollis promotes throughout—"I am not what happened to me. I am what I choose to become"—to extricate oneself from a purely historical vision of self with a grateful eye to the future.

How appropriate that Hollis chose for the title a snippet of the final line from the poem "Passing Through" by Stanley Kunitz, written when he was seventy-nine. How liberating and solidly universal is this sentiment of life's temporary nature, and it's precisely why it should be cherished. James Hollis has lived and taught through this prism for much of his life as a healer and a guide so others could incorporate it as a beacon that lights the seas of our journey both night and day.

DENNIS PATRICK SLATTERY, PHD

Dennis Patrick Slattery, PhD, is Distinguished Emeritus Professor in Mythological Studies at Pacifica Graduate Institute in Carpinteria, California. His most recent book titles are *The Way of Myth: Stories' Subtle Wisdom* and *The Fictions in Our Convictions: Essays on the Cultural Imagination.* dennispatrickslattery.com

Impermanence is life's
only promise to us,

And she keeps it with
ruthless impeccability.

—Jennifer Wellwood

PREFACE

Living with Borrowed Dust

In the past five years I have had elective knee and hip replacements; non-elective cancer treatments involving surgery, radiation, and chemotherapy; deep vein thrombosis (DVT) surgery; and two major spinal operations as the vertebrae of my spine dissolved and fractured, possibly as a result of the cancer treatment; additionally, my pelvis is now attached to my spine by bolts. So these recent days have been pain-ridden and cramped by various procedures, to say the least, especially since I continued to work as a psychoanalyst when out of the hospital. As a result of my uncertain medical prognosis, my wife and I recently moved to a retirement cooperative. Through it all, I found that my dicey medical situation was less on my mind than my work with analytic psychology. Even I found that surprising, and I can only conclude that the work of Carl Jung and psychodynamic psychology continue to animate, direct, and feed the life of the soul—at least this soul. If that were not the case, I would be spending my days collecting stamps or knitting doilies, or I'd probably be dead.

While analytic psychology remains on the periphery of modern psychological modalities, it never troubles me that analytically oriented therapists are such a small group, comparatively speaking. If we are doing what is right for ourselves and our clients, then deeper work provides compensation for the focus on mere symptom relief that our culture values so highly rather than the problem of meaning, which I believe undergirds most psychopathology. When we are separated from our own souls, there is a terrible suffering that inevitably spills into the world, into relationships, onto children, and into the world at large.

As Jung pointed out, neurosis is suffering that has not yet found its meaning. He does not rule out suffering, of course, but he does remind us that experiencing the meaning of our troubled transit helps us through difficult times. The Jungian model asks a lot of a person, but the reward is also substantial. As I have said to more than one client, our work is not about curing you, for you are not a disease, but it is a summons to a deeper dialogue that will make your life more interesting and will likely take you to spiritual landscapes where you hadn't planned to visit, yet each will bring a richer, darker hue to the course of your life.

When I look back at the beginning of my career, in my days as a professor of humanities, I began teaching Jung because I thought his understanding of symbolic formation was illuminating. When the psyche blessed me with a midlife depression and I had my first hour of analysis, something in me began to realize that my understanding of Jung's concepts was superficial. Until they became flesh, until they were modes of reflection on life as it is really lived, they remained what Alfred North Whitehead called merely "a bloodless dance of categories."

As a part of my training, I worked in a state psychiatric hospital part-time for three years. Serving on a locked ward, I was told to wear a tie so I would be identified as staff and allowed out in the evening. The magnitude of human suffering experienced in that hospital percolated through the layers of my life. As a child with various medical issues, I had grown up both fascinated by and frightened of hospitals. The older doctor to whom I had been assigned took me to see an autopsy. For days thereafter I saw that distended body and realized that my own psyche had somehow engineered me back into that world that I had fled as a youth. As I shared my experience with my analyst back in Zürich, he replied succinctly, "When you have faced your own fears, the fears of others will not be so difficult."

Shortly after that, I helped a doctor suture the face of a man who had had a chair thrown at him. I could not help but be impressed with the wisdom, the autonomy of the psyche that had subtly pulled me back into the world I had fled for the tempting refuge of the mind. Incredible as it may seem, my psyche was seeking its healing by returning me to the place of trauma. Now I was strong enough to take it on and find its meaning in a way my child self could not. As we know, fear is natural and normal, but a life governed by fear is something else. Today I see that hospital internship as a truly personal introduction to the healing intention of the psyche.

Along with many others in analysis, I learned to honor the world of dreams, of active imagination, and begin to ask questions such as "But what is that choice in service to inside?" A simple enough question, but it begins the forensic deepening. The problem with the unconscious is that it is unconscious.

Recently, while in the hospital, I was asked by a nurse what I did for a living.

"How does that work differ from ordinary psychology?" she asked.

"Well, for one thing, we try to evoke a conversation with the unconscious."

She thought awhile and replied, "Oh, I get it. You work with folks in a coma." The more I reflected on her comment, the more sense it made, for all of us, most of the time, are in altered states.

That is to say, we are driven by fears, responding to life's challenges with routinized and reflexive behaviors and largely unaware of the vast psychodramas coursing beneath the surface.

Amid the noise, we all intuit, deep down, that we have a "soul"—that is, some deep, deep place within that knows us better than we know ourselves, that abides throughout the course of this raggedy journey.

During the last half-century, I have been devoted to bringing the insights, attitudes, and practices of analytic psychology to as many people as possible through the venues of teaching, writing, and private praxis. This is hardly a job; rather, it is a "calling." If I think something is good for me, why would I not share it with others? As a result, what I have observed is that many folks are hungry for the life of the psyche and are willing to face the fire and open themselves to change. Even if popular culture itself is a vast panoply of distractions from the life of the soul, there are many who know something vital is missing in all that flash, flair, and razzmatazz. Behind the noise and beneath the surface, something in the soul of each of us cries out; something hums with the tension of expectation. While we may be distracted from this summons or unable to attend its entreaty, the soul keeps asking that we pay attention. Those moments of summons come to us through our symptomatology, in our dreams, and even in those difficult hours of sleeplessness.

In the chapters that follow, I examine and critique our preoccupation with seeking what to do and be from outside sources—for example, how to be "happy." But even then, something within us knows better and refuses to cooperate. What I rather wish to identify in the pages that follow are some of the tools we can use to undertake a deepened conversation with our souls. By examining how the conditions of collective culture affect us, either by supporting our journey or, more likely, providing more noise to crowd out our summons, we can begin to grow into our separate yet sometimes convergent journeys.

Amid the noise, we all intuit, deep down, that we have a "soul"—that is, some deep, deep place within that knows us better than we know ourselves, that abides throughout the course of this raggedy journey, and that offers us moments of respite, some solace, and considerable guidance for the governance of life. Having lost contact with that source within, we are at the mercy of the thousands of adaptations we required and acquired in childhood, including our overwhelming self-doubt, and the loudest banging noises assailing us from without.

So let this book be a companion, a summons, a guide, and a reminder that we carry within what we are so anxiously looking for in the crazed world out there. Let this book remind you of what you intuitively knew as a child but forgot or set aside as the promptings, demands, and incursions of the world took over. Let this book be a friend who wishes to travel with you as your life unfolds. Let it connect you once again to the wisdom our distant ancestors respected. And let it bring to you renewed purpose, depth, and dignity for this mysterious journey we call life.

JAMES HOLLIS, PHD
Washington, DC

Our business in life is not
to succeed, but to continue
to fail in good spirits.

—Robert Louis Stevenson

1

Happiness

Find What You Love and Let It Kill You

In Jack Gilbert's poem "A Brief for the Defense," the speaker surveys a world of sorrow, violence, starvation, and isolation, where even in the darkest of hours, there are moments of reprieve, moments of laughter, moments of improbable freedom of the human spirit.[1] The speaker says that amid the plethora of miseries, we also have to risk the gladness, even the joy, that may rise from living amid "the ruthless furnace of the world." Gilbert ends the poem with a plea that we remember the pleasures of certain moments here and there amid the suffering, which are just as real, just as compelling, just as defining in our journey as the suffering. Sometimes, there really is a moment of gladness in "the ruthless furnace of the world."

Those lines of poetry were written by someone who understands that if we don't grab this moment of respite, refuge, and regeneration, it will not come again. This fungible flesh that serves, as Shakespeare's Richard II noted, as "paste and cover to our bones," is truly borrowed, and the longer we live, the more the source of our borrowing seems to reclaim its loan to us.

During this brief loan transaction we call our life, we are told to be happy. I, for one, have tried earnestly and have occasionally been flush with happiness, and yet happiness as the goal or purpose of life does not speak to me of anything authentic. So I am pleased to be here in this imaginal space with you and reflect on this elusive and evanescent thing we call "happiness."

So how can these two points be true at the same time? We live in "the ruthless furnace of the world," *and* we are told to be happy. As a hospital nurse said to me before a recent painful procedure, "Go to your Happy Place now." I told her, respectfully, "This *is* my Happy Place." I was trying to be mindful of her good intentions and my battered but realistic view of the world at the same time. In that sentence, "This *is* my Happy Place," I experience pain, but I also do not forget the lighter hours life sometimes brings us. So, concomitantly, in those lighter hours, I also do not forget that somewhere, someone is suffering.

One of Samuel Beckett's characters, while waiting for a chap who never shows up, notes that the quantity of tears is a constant in the world. In order for someone to be laughing over here, someone has to be weeping over there. This line of reasoning may depress you, but it is a very Jungian challenge—to hold the tensions of opposites and honor the claims of both sides. Any view, any practice that sides with one value at the cost of the other leads to bad ends of one sort or another.

So, what is this thing called "happiness"? Is happiness ontological? That is, does it exist in and for itself in some recognizable form? If it has some ontic form, is it a noun? If a noun, what does it look like? Is it hiding somewhere, like South Dakota, and if we are clever enough, can we all figure that out and move there? We certainly spend a lot of time imagining that "happiness" will be found in a new car, a new home, a new partner. Can we ever figure out a surefire path to happiness? Or should we even try? The novelist Gustav Flaubert once concluded, "To be stupid, and selfish, and to have good health are three requirements for happiness, though if stupidity is lacking, the others are useless."[2]

The last thing I want to be known as is the guy who is against happiness, so I'd better explain myself a bit further. I devoutly wish for your happiness, for mine, for that of my children and all of everybody's children who walk the planet, but I have learned not to hold my breath that I, they, we will ever arrive at a steady state called "happiness" and abide there till the curtain falls on the last scene of this tawdry melodrama we have mounted on history's stage for all these turbulent centuries.

Some folks are unhappy that they are not permanently happy. Often, those who use social networks like Facebook see how happy other people seem to be, and they end up feeling miserable in comparison—being therein the witness to how happy their friends are with their fabulous children and their glorious times together. Not too many put the other side of their stories online, and so we tend to assume *they* are successful at this Happiness Game and we are not.

Let me describe a photo of a fellow who seems rather happy.[3] This baby is smiling and looking completely content. Isn't he blissful? Isn't he at the top of his game? He is so content that he cannot imagine he has a train of trouble, a train having left Newark at 6:45 and traveling at 86.4 miles per hour, headed right toward him. Since he is yet to take the math class to help him figure out when the train arrives at his door, we can allow him to remain happy as a clam. But, as far as we know, clams are not very conscious. It is consciousness and our imaginative capacity to summon up competing portraits of reality that combine to bring difficult hours to our vexed sleep. In Fleur Adcock's poem "Things," the speaker is awakened and surrounded by all the "things" that cause her distress. But for all her efforts to assuage the troubling visitations of guilt, anxiety, and dread, everything she fears gathers about her bed and collectively grows worse and worse and worse.[4] Who does not recognize those assaults by worry that have a habit of arriving in the ghostly hours of predawn?

But how often do we ask the question: Are we meant to be happy? If I am so meant, and am not happy, is there something wrong with me? Being happy does not seem to be a large consideration for most of the animal kingdom. A place to sleep, protection from predators, and food to forage seems to be enough to still their instinctual needs. But this human animal remains bewitched, bothered, and bewildered by the messiness of it all.

While studying in Switzerland, I was able to rent a lawyer's apartment to use as a consulting room while he was at work. He came home early once to find someone weeping and later asked me why I would ever want to spend my time with crying people. I didn't tell him about the time I was invited to an autopsy during my internship at the psychiatric hospital. That didn't make me happy, but I was happy to learn more about how the body fits together and how autopsies work. I think I did tell him it made me happy, and humbled, to be invited to be present with the suffering of others, but I don't think he got that, and so our conversation changed thereafter to deliberate and trivial banter.

My point here is that perhaps life is meaningless, but we are meaning-seeking creatures who are driven to understand it. Failing that, we attempt to form some meaningful relationship to life. We learn from archetypal psychology, from the core of primal religious experiences, from quantum physics, and from the artist's eye that all is energy. Matter itself is a dynamic, temporary arrangement of energy. (As Pierre Teilhard de Chardin observed, matter is spirit slowed enough to be visible.) Apparently, a religious symbol or prayer, a work of art, or an expressive practice can act on our psyche and channel that energy when it has been blocked, deadened, or split off. Meaning makes life bearable and is the gift of being here in "the ruthless furnace of the world." As that effervescent philologist of Basel Friedrich Nietzsche once observed, the person who has a "why" can live with any "how."

Apparently, though, the concept of happiness has a lot of sales value. One never sees a glum family driving off with a new Toyota. During the commercials for *Jeopardy!*, one can view all the new dread diseases that await the elderly and all the wonderfully named meds that are titrated to cure them while providing tons of new side effects by way of a speed reader. And we have Positive Psychology, designed to emphasize right thinking and right conduct. The emergence of this fashionable approach to life is especially American in its mentality. The American "Can Do" attitude, allied with muscular efforts to achieve one's goals, will reportedly bring about happiness and a sense of well-being. Brother Job, from over two and a half millennia ago, is not welcome in the precincts of the privileged, but he was the original positive psychologist who thought right thinking and right practice would lead to abundance and well-being. (I won't tell you what happened to him.)

One of the most popular classes at Yale, The Science of Well-Being, taught by Dr. Laurie Santos, is described as "reveal[ing] misconceptions about happiness, annoying features of the mind that lead us to think the way we do, and the research that can help us change."[5] The student is enjoined to incorporate new behaviors and expect new outcomes. No wonder this is such a popular course for unhappy undergraduates who are convinced they can fix not only this problem but also the rest of society's problems.

Perhaps the utopian vision of building a life of happiness would be not only possible but desirable for all of us if the universe would only cooperate. If right attitudes and practices could keep that cell from metastatic incursion, or find that bolt on the roller coaster before the car slips off the rail, or prevent that child from walking in front of a car . . . But suffering comes to all of us. Perhaps in her phrase "annoying features of the mind," Professor Santos is intuiting the presence of those noisome complexes we all acquire along the way. And yes, they can and must be challenged lest we be locked into misery. Every complex is a defense of a perception, a fractal worldview, generated by the demands of the hour when they were formed. Different forces produce different message centers in all of us, but we all have our appointments with disappointment, betrayal, grief, and loss.

So much of what we call "happiness" is contextual. Did those who attended the clashes of the gladiators have thoughts about the lives sacrificed before them, or did they open a box of popcorn and enjoy the spectacle? (Do we so remember, watching the NFL, that their young bodies are being destroyed for our diversion? I do.) For a thirsty person, a drink of water is momentary happiness. Consider this story. A man is crawling across the desert. He finally comes across a stand in the desert selling ties. "What would I want with a tie?" he jeers the peddler. Finally, on his last legs, he climbs a hillock and sees a rich, lush green oasis with fountains of water gushing everywhere. Summoning his last strength, he rushes to the entrance, whereupon a guard stops him and says, "I am sorry, sir, but you have to have a tie to enter here."

Do we define the absence of suffering as "happiness"? Are the various avenues of narcosis—drugs, alcohol, materialism—a way of dealing with this problem through numbing and distraction? Is the question of "happiness" to be put aside and sorted out in an afterlife, which, at best, would be *another* life and not this miserable one? What forms of denial or wish fulfillment or moral vacuity are necessary to achieve a happy hour in the midst of such a world as ours? In fact, during Happy Hour, do we get happy or just numbed to the intensity of it all? For a person to live in a semipermanent state of happiness, it seems necessary to have a capacity for denial, repression, and the ready impulse to look the other direction. Such a life would tend to be fugitive rather than engaged, with the superficial crowding out the depths where authenticity lies. Such a life is a constant wish to have the anabasis without the catabasis, the mountaintop peak experience without the prerequisite initiatory descent into the depths.

> What suffering brings to us most is the query that Jung proposed each of us consider: "What supports you when nothing supports you?"

As mentioned in the preface, I spent about as much time in hospitals and rehabilitation clinics over the past two years as I did outside. I had many opportunities to reflect on Jung's late-life definition of "God." When he was asked to clarify and expand his offhand comment in his famous 1959 BBC interview that he did not "believe" in God because he "knew" God, Jung elaborated, and I paraphrase, "I call God that which flings itself violently across my path and alters my conscious intentions for good or for ill." In being treated for two cancers in a very aggressive protocol, and then finding the bones of my spine fracturing and leading to risky surgeries, I had and have many an hour with pain, and with many continuing questions. I considered Jung's heretical definition provocative and helpful because it requires the ego to reframe its pictures of the world, its agenda, and its expectations. Instead of asking, as I did at first, how quickly do I regain my life as I knew it—full of travel and thoughtful folks to meet around the world—I was brought to ask: What can I do with these greatly reduced capacities to serve the values I most treasure, sustain an equitable presence in marriage, and live with an uncertain prognosis that may kick in with crippling or lethal blows at any moment? Balance that with the Buddhist reminder that suffering rises from our resistance to reality, which is compounded by our attachment to our desires and phantasies about how the world *should* be rather than how it is. The more we cling to these phantasies, the more happiness will elude us.

I am blessed that I have a caring and constant spouse, my wife, Jill, and she played a large role in my resilience and recovery. But it was a struggle, which I depict in this poem I wrote after the last surgery.

The Lady with the Lamp

I once was so afraid of doctors that I decided to be one,
thinking I would learn secrets to stand up to the fear.
Without knowing it, I did my best to distance myself
from the odious kingdom of pain,
the ravening body that leeches the soul.

At midlife I left academia and retrained as a psychoanalyst.
While working in a psychiatric hospital, my mentor, grizzled
sergeant of wars past, said, "Come with me, Hollis, I have
a patient you would work well with."
We entered a room filled with observers. On the table below
was Guernica, or so I thought. I assembled the splayed organs
until the form of a woman took its place. The old sergeant's joke
apparent now. What I had run from was staring through me.
As Jung put it, what is denied inwardly
comes to us in outer form, and we call it fate.

Now, these decades later, I have returned from hospital again.
Covered with scars from operations, burned from radiation,
clanking with prostheses made in factories somewhere,
I ache for reprieve. I didn't want to leave Jill alone,
so I came home again, until the next time. Through it all,
her face summoned me across the fog-ridden, shroud-laden sea
to this stupefying ignorant world
where bludgeons and scalpels perform their daily office.

What suffering brings to us most is the query that Jung proposed each of us consider: "What supports you when nothing supports you?" What a wonderful, heuristic question! It will be with us the rest of our lives, for sooner or later we will be flung back upon ourselves. While I am most grateful to modern medical science and the loving support of friends and family, there are many dark hours where we are wholly alone and must consider the radical question life brings to us: How now will you live your life when it is not yours to control?

The chief side effect of our social conditioning, and the thousand necessary adaptations of childhood to a world it cannot manage, is the progressive erosion of our instinctual guidance, that within which tells us what is right for us and gives us the strength to persevere in the presence of suffering and defeat.

A couple of years ago, while doing a Zoom-cast with a London host, I was asked whom in history I would most like to interview. Having been raised in Springfield, Illinois, my first thought was Abraham Lincoln. My second was Lou Gehrig, whom I had idolized in my childhood, little knowing then what Lou Gehrig's disease was. But then I thought, most of us would leap at the chance to go back and talk to ourselves as a ten-year-old. We now know what that child most needed: modeling, mentoring, instruction, affirmation, and most of all permission to feel what he really feels and to risk what is rising from within and asking for expression. He needs to be told that he is already equipped by nature for the trials of life, and if he trusts himself, hangs in there, he will come out the other side of those conflicts. He needs to be told that his fears are normal and natural, but that he is still summoned by life to live as fully as possible in the face of that fear. He needs to know that Other within is his real self and that honoring that dear soul, and risking its imperative in the ruthless furnace of this world, will be his lifelong task.

From time to time, you may share that child with others, but mostly you are to begin a lifelong conversation with that child and create the ways in which he or she may explore and express that soul's desire for joy, for creativity, for exuberance of many kinds. And, even more, the adult needs to remember that, in a forest of bewildering choices and tension-fraught costs, that child's intuitive knowing is also the long-sought compass needle for finding true north through the darkest and coldest of hours.

When we risk the journey, something rises within to support and direct us, some deep knowing of the way—even when we are most lost. If that first step into the unknown is not taken, something within will never be birthed into this world. If one is only seduced by the known, the possible children will remain in the closet forever, and one's earthly children will have to clear out that closet for us.

To each of us, this call rises with each dawn and awaits our decision. As brother Hamlet put it succinctly, "To be or not to be: that is the question." No one can escape or evade that question without something dying within. Whatever small chip we were entrusted to bring to the great mosaic of life remains hidden, and the whole is forever diminished by our timorous spirit.

But where, you may ask, is our esteemed "happiness" in all this? Do we not recognize that our nervous concern with happiness has been absorbed into a larger frame of discussion? The issue of happiness is legitimate and will not go away. But it *does* get reframed.

Trusting that inner voice will inevitably bring one into conflict with the world, beginning in the family of origin. One is never spared that conflict, for conflict lies at the heart of life's dynamics. Something in the unconscious is forever seeking conscious expression and is certainly not wishing to be neglected for a lifetime.

This voice is the voice of the soul. The noisy and noisome complexes surely have voices as well, but there is a larger voice that supersedes them. One complex voice cries out, "Security at all costs!" but does not comprehend that the price of security is the larger demand going unheard, unattended. We just didn't show up when called to life. Another voice cries out, "Try to fit in!" not understanding that this seductive need will sabotage the expression of the soul, the good being the enemy of the better. Another voice laments, "But I will be so alone," not knowing then, and perhaps never, that when one has a living dialogue with the soul, one is never alone. There is always a rich and engaged presence that satisfies the question "What supports us when nothing supports us?"

I do not think we are here to follow our bliss, our infantilizing desires for someone to take care of us, our narcissistic phantasies of totality. We only get a small part of it, if that, and real life asks something more of us. Perhaps it is better expressed to say, "Follow your passion," as long as you recall that "passion" derives from the Latin *passio*, which means "to suffer." Even moments of high achievement arrive with suffering as the necessary companion. What matters so much to you that you suffer its demands upon you, yet the service of which enriches your journey? Perhaps, we may conclude, the object of life is not to be successful, or to be happy, but to discern and serve that which is worthy of our service.

So we move through this life, exploring alpine meadows of joy and spontaneity, balanced by compensatory excursions into the savannahs of suffering. That voice, the voice of the soul, speaks to us each day, quietly. If we ignore it long enough, it will roar thunderously in our ears. If we still ignore it, it will burst through our front door, though we will ascribe its presence to fate rather than the sum of our unconscious choices that built into a world of consequences.

In the end, life expects to consume us. Desire once meant the star that guided the mariner across the tempest-tossed seas. Desire is what gets us into trouble, and trouble is where the soul is most manifest. If we wish to live fully, it is not happiness that is the goal, but to be consumed by that which we have come to love. Happiness as a goal is too small a piece of the whole, though it is often on the periphery of the most difficult of struggles.

The voice speaks to us daily and says, "Rise, show up, step into the world once more. You will get knocked down again, but this is where your life is meant to take you. The soul and the world are waiting to see you once brave, once ready to take it all on again, up once more for the day's struggle." The Greek novelist Nikos Kazantzakis once wrote of his prayer to God: "My prayer is the report of a soldier to his general: This is what I did today, this is how I fought to save the entire battle in my own sector, these are the obstacles I found, this is how I plan to fight tomorrow."[6]

The soul serves the ministries of the invisible world and, from time to time, may even prove the builder of institutions, the shaper of collective will, to acknowledge the invisible and its demands. (As Jung noted, exploring the meaning of the great Cathedral of Cologne is not to be understood as a discourse on mineralogy.) If you risk enough, you will be blessed by the soul killing you, but remember to thank her. She brought you into this world; she has animated its cerements with the red flush of life; and she has brought you on your journey.

If sometimes you lie broken and bereft, no matter. She calls and will keep calling. Trust that the voice in the dark woods will continue to call you and leave breadcrumbs in the forest daily for you to follow. Ultimately, she will kill you, but she also has given you the best parts of your life. So rise from slumber, find what you love, and let it kill you. And then, from time to time, you may find yourself, to your astonishment, happy . . . for a while.

2

Meta

Beyond, After, Across, Before

When Facebook felt the heat of public and regulatory criticism, it transformed into Meta. Nothing like slipping from a ship in peril to a new one just launched. *Meta* is a Greek word, meaning "after, beyond, among, behind," and can be found in common words like "metaphysics," "metabolism," "metaphor," and so on. Literally, "metaphor" means "to carry over;" thus the meaning is carried over from A to B. To say, "I was a tired cowboy" after strenuous activity is clear enough, even if one does not herd cattle for a living. "We are the eyelids of defeated caves"—Allen Tate's metaphor in the poem "An After-Dinner Speech"—communicates, somewhat obscurely, that what is knowable in one realm is a bridge to an unknowable realm, illuminating what might otherwise be unapproachable. Similarly, Facebook as an entity no longer has to bear the investigative heat and, may we say, conveniently metamorphizes into something else entirely.

When working with clients in a psychoanalytic capacity, one generally encounters resistance of one kind or another. On the more overt front, sometimes folks will simply avoid topics they know carry some heat or are related to something they would rather not address. Even more commonly, the client frequently reports their disappointment with themselves for falling into the same nonproductive behaviors that drove them to therapy in the first place. While it is true that we can and must hold ourselves accountable for change, non-change, and the outcomes of both, we need to remember that beneath the panoply of behaviors courses a more archaic story that one might call a meta-story, or meta-complex. While this meta-story may or may not be conscious to us, its effect is evident, persistent, and pernicious.

But first, a word about complexes. I surmise that of all of Jung's contributions to our understanding of the workings of the psyche, perhaps the most consistently useful is the idea of the "complex." Briefly, a complex is a charged experience that resides in our psyche and, when triggered, has the power to usurp the ego state and enact its historic "message." While the term was coined by Berlin psychiatrist Theodore Ziehen in 1898, Jung developed its importance. Working with the Association Experiment at the Burghölzli Klinik in Zürich,[1] Jung noted that ordinary citizens following the protocol experienced disturbances of consciousness from the mere recitation of words. Similarly, in his medical school dissertation, he pondered how a medium could dissociate from ego control and let "voices" emanate from and pass through her. In both areas it became clear that there were clusters of energy separate from ego awareness, or at least ego control, that, when triggered, had the power to usurp the ego state and enact its agenda.

When people query why they acted in a certain way during conflict or say "I don't know what came over me" or "I lost control for a while," they are acknowledging the presence of these dissociative clusters of energy. We all have them, for we all have histories and have acquired certain charged areas of our psychic life that abide with us wherever we may go, and however long we may be going there. The awakened consciousness becomes aware of those presences, sometimes the hard way, and thereafter begins to factor in the rich choral presence that lives within. Over several decades Jung variously identified complexes as "splinter psyches," "little people," "revolting vassals in an empire," "skeletons in the cupboard," "tyrannical usurpers of consciousness," "shadow governments of the ego," "goblins," and "separate personalities." Or, as one thoughtful analyst began each session, "Let me tell you what the kids have been doing this week."

Just as we say that people "in love" are mad, distracted, and possessed, so we may see that the rough edges of reality will sooner or later wear away the patina of illusion, and the reality of the other will emerge. We may say, with a small measure of hyperbole, that when we are in a complex, we are transiently and metaphorically "psychotic." Who has not momentarily been possessed by rage or perhaps frozen by shame? After the complex has spun its thread and exhausted its energy, it falls back into the unconscious, whereupon we are left to deal with its consequences.

And now back to the main thread of meta. Every complex has a quantum of energy, a fragmentary script, a somatic manifestation, and a distorting vision of reality. Most of them are harmless enough, although their constant iteration begins to show up as what philosopher Ludwig Wittgenstein described as *Lebensformen*, or "life patterns," whether intended or not. It is even clear that much of daily life is the rolling out of these complexes, which reinforces their autonomous power and their capacity to manage much of our life for us. How conscious we are at any given hour is dubious. How often we are routinely subservient to these charged messages of history is the ongoing project of personal inquiry, whether in therapy or not.

Much of one's project of self-awareness begins and ends with the mere identification of these complexes at work in one's daily life, but seldom do we consider that there may be even deeper forces that govern the complexes themselves. If we may say that each complex is a story about self, world, and their interactions, we may also acknowledge that there are meta-stories that lie deeper within and constitute our entire engagement with life.

What, then, is a meta-complex? Well, a complex is formed as a result of the individual's effort to make some sense of any experience that befalls her or him. As such, it is not an objective view of the moment but a highly subjective reading that offers an interpretation and seeks to assemble some sort of role or reaction to the experience. This reading is of course unique to each person, which partly explains why two persons, say siblings with the same parents, house, and cereal in the morning, can have such different life patterns as they serve their own unique readings of life's jagged terrain. (Notice how differently two siblings may describe their family of origin and their formative experiences therein.)

If the experience of the moment is pleasant, nurturing, or protective, one tends to move toward it. Even if it is not, one's lifetime may be spent seeking to replicate it, unwittingly submitting to that archaic story as a defining presence in one's life. For example, in cases where the parents were warm, loving, and nurturing, the person naively expects those qualities in others. For many others, the opposite occurs. The primal objects, that is, parental figures, stand as virtual gods—powerful, omnipotent, and perhaps punitive or absent. But, typically, the dynamics, stratagems, and lessons of such experiences are internalized, become normative, and live on as a provisional life script.

Another core idea that is embedded in every person's psyche, albeit in infinite variations, revolves around the issue of trust. For those blessed with a nurturing and protective constancy, there may well be a certain level of naivete rising from an expectation that others will prove trustworthy in other times and places. For those who have been let down, their needs and interests betrayed, a generalized distrust, even paranoia, will prevail in the conduct of their lives. (Those who are parents know that one of the most difficult decisions of parenting involve figuring out to what degree we should protect our children or allow them to experience the inevitable wounds of the world. Overprotection leads to naivete and immature development, and insufficient protection leads to traumatic incursions that debilitate and scar them.)

A few examples may prove illustrative. Every child, from infancy to old age, attempts to read the world and find its message with archaic but vital questions, such as: Are you going to be there reliably or not? Can I count on you to do what you say you are going to do? What am I to do when you do not do as expected or desired? What does it say about you, or perhaps me, if you don't? Similarly, your behaviors toward me, or lack thereof, underline in me a provisional definition of me. Am I, as I am, worthy of your interest or not? Even though you may be worn out, tired, or distracted by your own problems, your absence will be interpreted as suggesting I am unworthy of your interest. How then will I conduct myself in subsequent human relationships? Will I stay away from intimacy so I don't replicate that hurt? Will I rifle through relationships as I desperately look for a better mirror of my needs, only to find, typically, the same old outcome as a result of my inherent needfulness? Will I ever stop and realize that my troubled relationships are a function of my meta-story, which keeps imposing itself upon my outer possibilities?

The famous 1781 painting *The Nightmare* by Swiss painter Henry Fuseli dramatically renders an encounter with the powers of the unconscious that sometimes come to us in dreams.[2] It dramatizes a state of possession by the contents of the depths. While not as dramatic as Fuseli's painting, a patient, Naomi, also entered a kind of possession. The story goes that she was a child in a large, impoverished family in which she was drafted to be a surrogate parent to help with younger siblings. Her own needs and entitlement to the good things in life were wholly unmet. In later life, when she had acquired much wealth and benefits, she experienced an identity crisis when she and her husband separated. As a result, she fell back upon the old impoverishment story and became vindictive, grasping, mendacious, and possessed by a need to get what had been denied earlier. Any thought of fairness or reciprocity went out the window as she hid money, lied under oath, and sought to recover what she believed she was meant to have. Rather than live the old wound of loss, deprivation, and humiliation, she seized control of her situation, albeit in ways inconsistent with her professed values. She was not psychotic in the clinical sense, but she was possessed by an old story that she was determined to rewrite at any cost. Her elemental sense of reality and reciprocity was supplanted by vindictiveness, greed, and the desire to dominate and destroy the other who had let her down. Her estranged partner even had dreams of her domination of him, as his psyche internalized the new person she had become. It was not that she was a new person; rather, she had, by virtue of a meta-story, become the person of old who was dedicated to no longer being a victim.

The shaking of foundations, such as what divorce can cause, set the old narrative to rise, metaphorically sit on her chest, and usurp the present reality.

So it is when a meta-story rises to take charge of conscious life for the length of its programmed energy. Just as Scarlett O'Hara swears in *Gone with the Wind* that she will never be impoverished again, and becomes a grasping, driven vixen, so too did Naomi become the opposite of that poor child she once was. Now, at great cost to her adult children and erstwhile partner, and losing her warmth and generosity, she began to serve an avenging and restitutive angel who rose to defend her. The meta-story had coursed beneath the surface for so long, and, when push came to shove, had seized its day—making everyone a victim. Once powerless, she was, like Scarlett O'Hara, owned by power, but it was a delusive pseudo-power deriving from the old narrative.

I have written elsewhere of two men in their fifties who had ploughed through three marriages, each one destroyed by their fears of abandonment. Both of them, around ten years of age, had seen their mother leave with a strange man and never return. Thus, their meta-story rose from those psychic ashes: "If I cannot count on her, why should I be able to count on you?" Though flawed in its extrapolation, it is a logical outcome of that traumatic loss, but it predictably led to what Freud called the "repetition compulsion." The autonomy of their meta-story was such that it trapped each of them in an inordinate suspicion of their spouses, even tapping their phones and, in one case, demanding a polygraph after a detective had failed to produce evidence of infidelity. In their core, the child's fears of abandonment were so great that they became the de facto lens through which both men saw each of their partners. In time, their partners could not bear the weight of constant suspicion and scrutiny and ended the marriages, inadvertently ratifying and reinforcing the message of the meta-story: "See, she could not be trusted, and this one is just like *her*, just as I feared."

In both examples, the actual identity of the person, with all her or his capacity for different choices, and the natural resilience of maturation were supplanted by the archaic message "They let you down then, and they are surely going to do it again and again." How sad it proves when not only the individual but also their partners and children are victimized by the power of the meta-story that metastasizes history and repeats its tragic outcomes.

"What is this path really in service to inside of me?" If I don't ask that question, I may be fairly certain that I am on autopilot again and in service to the meta-story.

In another clinical example, Cynthia was the go-to person in her family and social organizations. Everyone would agree that she followed through on assignments, never demurred, and never complained. Obviously, she enjoyed all these commitments. But did anyone ever ask her if this was the case? Did Cynthia ask Cynthia how she *really* felt about her life? Cynthia's first response to such interrogations was a ready profession of delight or, at least, acceptance of such expectations from others. The truth is, Cynthia's life was a prison from which she could not escape. In other words, Cynthia could not really trust herself for honesty about these matters.

The first child of a troubled marriage, she learned early to assume responsibilities while her immature parents continued to battle each other. If they were not going to be playing their assigned roles as the adults on the scene, she would have to fill the vacuum. She would perform their unfinished business, or distract them with humor, or compensate for the generalized gloom of the house with her academic and athletic achievements. Everyone loved Cynthia, everyone expected much from her, and no one, including Cynthia, would tumble to the fact that she was a forlorn child doing the best she could because others around her were not. In Cynthia's case, her work with her dreams was what opened history's casket. Repeatedly, her dreams brought up emotionally fraught situations from childhood that left her exhausted, frightened, and on edge. Her assumption of the responsibility for the work of so many others meant she had no real time of her own or permission to kick back and relax. When she began to explore the meta-story that coursed beneath the surface of her life and realized its systemic hold on her, her first thought was to flee to the South Pacific and leave all projects behind. This understandable phantasy was, of course, just as ungrounded. What would be more difficult for her proved to be the middle path' namely, to stay in the fire and not run from it. What she needed to learn, and learn she slowly did, was to say no, to get in someone's face who was dumping more and more on her, and to ask herself from situation to situation, "What do I really feel about this? What do I really want to do?" Of course, in real life we don't always get to do what we really want to do, but if we don't from time to time, we are living not *our* lives but someone else's.

When Jung noted that the greatest burden every child faces is the unlived life of the parents, he might as well have been speaking of Cynthia. I am pleased to report that her sustained effort at sorting through the motives of any given situation led her to a more robust and satisfying life. As I have indicated elsewhere, we all have to ask the question of any choice, at any juncture, "What is this path really in service to inside of me?" If I don't ask that question, I may be fairly certain that I am on autopilot again and in service to the meta-story, working its way through the layers of my psyche and imposing itself on my freedom to choose.

Each of us, even as infants and as children, nervously scans the horizon for clues about what is coming next. This is how our species survived the approach of the lion, or enemies, or inhospitable familial settings. But, of course, the child's interpretation, the readings life necessitates, are subjective and tied to that time and place. Accordingly, when applied to other settings, other people, and the new present, the message of the old meta-stories tends to prejudice the outcomes and add another layer to the weight of history upon the new hour. Even something as important as the choice of a partner may either be a repetition of the dynamics of the old story or a flight from it. Never assume that the old story is not present in such choices. Without awareness, we repeat our fated histories or we run from them; either way, we serve the meta-story. I must confess that when I see a couple at the altar, I cannot help but wonder what stories brought them together, dictate their reflexive interactions, and perhaps even adumbrate their future outcomes. One has to ask, if we are unaware of the presence and insistence of the story beneath the story, just how much freedom do we have in these immense choices with immense consequences?

From time to time, one becomes aware: "I have been here before," and with that simple recognition the possibility of shuffling off the chains of history emerges. Why do my relationships tend to turn out the same ways? What about my partner do I find both familiar and annoying? Why do I find myself discontented, adrift, and looking in all directions? These elemental questions are in fact profound and searching, and the failure to recognize that the common denominator in every relationship is oneself means that the iron wheel of history will turn once more, and the archaic story will grow stronger.

Meta-complexes or meta-stories are typically aligned along the core fault lines of existence. They are always addressing vital questions such as: Is the Other safe or unsafe? Can I trust the Other? Is the Other punitive, invasive, or abandoning? How am I viewed by the Other—as worthwhile or unworthy? What do I have to do to gain love and approval? Is it productive to move toward the Other or necessary to keep my distance? Do I have to twist myself into something other than what I am to please or gain the approval of the Other? What are the conditions I need to meet in order to fit in, be acceptable to others? And so on. These questions are tied not only to adaptation but, in many regards, to survival itself. No infant or child can survive without some sort of ongoing negotiation and set of adaptations with these environmental demands.

These demands are not only interpersonal but collective. Accordingly, poverty, war, chronic tension, systemic intrusions, and many other environmental disorders demand adaptation, sometimes even the annihilation of the inherent structures of childhood personality in order to survive. Is it any wonder then that the residuals of these early adaptations and micro-scripts circulate beneath the surface of the adult's life? Is it any wonder that so many repetitions in our lives emanate precisely from the paradox that what was once adaptive and necessary is later constrictive and binds one to the limitations that are found in a child's powerlessness? Does that person ever learn to say, "Where did *I* lose that object?" rather than "Who stole it?" Can one learn to open and listen rather than feel obliged to step in and fix it one more time?

In any given moment in an adult's life, the invisible hand of history reaches up and pulls the old lever, and the train of life goes down the well-worn track rather than unfolding a new and unique journey of life—a life that each child carries within as a desire and a possibility. Until we see these "hauntings," we remain their captive. But seeing them does not diminish their power. In fact, much of the second half of life is dedicated to the identification of these spectral presences and to combatting their regressive agendas. Out of the hammer blows of history a new life may be forged, but the anvil upon which it is shaped is the constant in a person's life. But the hovering presence of history, with its circumnavigating instructions, is truly the only constant, even as each of us seeks fuller expression in the smithy of freedom.

To the dismay of conscious life, meta-complexes and meta-stories run much, if not most, of our lives. The window of freedom is very narrow, and it is wholly closed if we forget for a moment their recondite wake running beneath the surface of daily life. To live with more intention, we must ask ourselves: What are my core perceptions of myself and others, and how might we relate to each other? When I survey the topography of my life thus far, what patterns are there, and to what meta-fictions are they in service? We do not do crazy things; we do logical things based on the "stories" activated intrapsychically.

So we start with the pattern, the eruption, the stuck place, and ask to what "idea" are they in service. Then, we take on that "idea" and, over time, seek to replace it with a more mature reading of the world now construed by a person who is no longer a child.

Which way I fly is Hell;
myself am Hell.

—John Milton

3

Filling Our House with Gold

Unbidden Ideas and Compelling Behaviors

One of the saddest notes in Western culture is the archetypal expulsion from Eden. If the Edenic phase suggests a life linked to instinct, home, and abundance, expulsion leads to exile, loneliness, and an aching desire for reconnection. (The etymology of the word "religion" expresses the desire for reconnection.) On a personal level, each infant is expelled from the womb and is more or less left to her or his own devices to survive a few decades. No wonder that child cries a lot and clings, clings, clings to whatever may offer a simulacrum of connection: a favored blanket, a familiar thumb, a ratty old toy. The child does not think such objects are the real deal, but she or he has learned to think symbolically, metaphorically. The bunny with tattered ears is available, constant, comforting, and the best one can manage in one's powerlessness.

We all have addictions, if one understands that an addiction is merely a reflexive anxiety management technique.

On the journey to follow, this deep need for connection will persist even as the person suffers loss after loss after loss. So it goes: attachment and loss, attachment and loss, attachment and loss. If we took this dilemma literally for a moment, we could imagine the person with numerous plugs extruding from the body and soul, all seeking to connect somewhere, anywhere that offers a crumb of solace, a hint of relief, or a hope of homecoming. Even as multitudes starve and food becomes both a scarcity and a fungible commodity, popular Western culture has created a vast panoply of resources that cry out their promise to connect, to nurture, to fill the emptiness felt within.

We have all seen pigs rutting in the trough. Similarly, the spectacle of hordes of souls shoving each other right and left on Black Friday to snag a flat-screen TV is surely a snapshot of this deep ache for connecting to something, even if it is a piece of metal and glass through which the reaches of desire are intimated. Teenagers who have their internet privileges abridged suffer all the withdrawal symptoms of the addict. Indeed, ours is an addictive culture. An addiction is a routinized, reflexive behavior designed to lower the level of distress at that moment. A chain smoker may consume several cigarettes or the bibulously inclined will quaff several drinks and be briefly comforted by the pleasant flush of gamma aminobutyric acid through the brain.

It's like the parable of King Midas, who, possessing more than most, still ached with emptiness, still longed for the reassurance that wealth could not provide. Given his Mephisphelean bargain with the gods, he got his wish. Imagine that! If we all got our wish, how much greater the expectation, how much greater the disappointment. You want gold? Well, here it is. Enjoy. And soon one realizes that the thing desired is merely a thing and, as such, has little to offer that is sustaining. Nothing is more evanescent than a need satisfied.

Midas, seeking to own that gold, is now owned by that gold, as anyone is who is caught in an addiction. We all have addictions, if one understands that an addiction is merely a reflexive anxiety management technique. One need not even realize that one is anxious, but the psyche knows, and the reflexive treatment plan is catalyzed and reinforced. Ironically, there are fewer horrors than needs satisfied, for then one still has to confront the spectacle of oneself in one's naked, unslaked desire and its unquenched hunger for satiety. Saint Augustine, a self-described libertine, prayed for release from his addiction and, failing over and over in his lubricious efforts, finally surrendered and concluded that the human heart is endlessly restless, and only finds its rest in a relationship with God. This idea, in fact, offered comfort and relief to many through the years, although today fewer and fewer moderns experience a similar surcease of longing. As one person put it, "I no longer believe in God, but I sure do miss Him."

It is clear from this wisdom that filling one's house with gold, or sex, or the latest shiny thing leads only to a sterility in which nothing means anything anymore. Such a condition is what haunts Western materialism. As the gods of the earth, the seas, and the air continue their withdrawal, we have religious fundamentalism as a panic-driven need to retain, restore, and rejuvenate a relationship that once linked folks to the transcendent realm. Sadly, the secret of fundamentalism, and we all have a fundamentalist somewhere inside us, is not reconnecting with the source as one hopes, but is rather an angst-driven urge that will never achieve a surfeit. This dirty little secret is why fundamentalism sits atop violence because its anxiety is so great that it will aggress against anything or anyone that reminds us of our essential isolation and disconnection.

Regardless of its various manifestations, "addiction" has become an ugly word, conjuring up ugly images: a car veering into the left lane, a person lying in the street, a shattered life. When we reflect on the two elements common to all addictions, we realize that addictive behaviors may be found in all of us, again from the idea that addictions are reflexive anxiety management systems. Each of those words is important.

Since no human is free of anxiety, we all have our habituated means of coping with anxiety, whether the disturbing affect is conscious or not. For example, many years ago I used to allow patients to smoke in the consulting room, thinking that they had enough stress in their lives without my adding to it. However, one couple, both chain smokers, lit one cigarette after another and, in a one-hour session, totaled twelve cigarettes, six apiece. I counted. The smoke and smell hung in the room for days, and from then on I changed my policy. And yet, if someone had asked them, "Did you smoke during the session?" both would have said, "Yes, I had a cigarette." In other words, their reflexive management of anxiety was so conditioned, so habituated, that neither thought about it and how systematized it had become in their lives.

I ask you now to stop and think about how you reflexively "manage" anxiety, or better, how you're repetitively managed *by* anxiety. The inner logic of an addictive pattern is that one suffers an unacceptable level of distress and, through connection with some "other," feels a momentary lowering of the disturbing affect. Say, for example, that while reading this, your room fills slowly with water, but your attention is so focused on the content of what you're reading that you do not attend to this event consciously. However, the psyche nonetheless takes note and seeks to lessen the disturbance. Through experiment and exploration each of us will solicit a behavior that lowers the water level, at least momentarily. The next time this happens, that earlier behavior will likely be repeated, whether consciously or not, and therein lies the addictive hook: the experience of momentary surcease of distress by a reflexive management system.

Connecting with the Other serves to lower the distress occasioned by our existential isolation, vulnerability, and dependencies. For many folks the Other is a substance: food, alcohol, purchasable material objects, a warm body. For others it is found through distractive "connections" with television, the internet, ideologies, compulsive prayer or mantras, and the like. For most of us, a common addictive pattern is so much at the heart of daily life that we seldom recognize its role in our psychological economy—namely, routine. Routinization is a means by which the familiar is imposed upon the uncertain. Notice how we get bent out of shape by the traffic jam at rush hour, when the paper arrives late, when our plotted schedule is interrupted. The magnitude of affect we suffer is disproportionate to the minor provocation, which is an indication of the arousal of anxiety.

The second key element of addiction is that our daily conscious life is repeatedly invaded by unbidden ideas. While these "ideas" are mostly unconscious, they have the power to stir anxiety within us. When a person clings to food, for example, he or she is in the grip of a powerful, existentially threatening idea; namely, "If I do not have this object, this comfort, in hand, what will be there for me in the darkness of this journey?" When we make this thought conscious, it may appear a peculiar, even ridiculous displacement of emotion onto matter, but in the symbolic world of the unconscious, the person's psyche has moved him or her to fasten onto an object, food, with its implied nurturing hope, as a stay against the anxiety in which we daily swim.

None of what we are discussing here is new, for addiction is as old as the human story. We find a notable and compelling portrait of a modern neurotic person like us in Shakespeare. The last thing we need to do is judge or shame any person for being human, for falling prey to the thousand natural shocks this flesh is heir to, as brother Hamlet put it four centuries ago. He is the same one who observed that he could be bounded in a nutshell and count himself a king of infinite space, if he did not have bad dreams. He also illustrates the "Hamlet complex" we all have— that there are things we know we should do, like give up an addiction, but for reasons we do not know, we do not or cannot.

What else are New Year's resolutions for but to set off valiantly to address the problems we are so keenly aware of, and why are we so likely to fail in our resolve? One of the reasons it is so difficult to break addictive patterns is because we are treating the reflexive behavior rather than the "idea" it was formed to treat. Since our management systems wrap themselves around our core anxieties—fear of loss of autonomy, fear of the magnitude of our journey, fear of abandonment, and the like—we never get to the real issue. If ever one is to address an addiction, one has to finally address the unbidden ideas to which our psyches and, therefore, our addictive strategies are in service. These "ideas" are not shameful, although the consequences of some of our management systems often produce shaming consequences for us and those around us.

The usual treatment plan for any addiction is a summons to a heroic will. The heroic will is certainly a great asset and few of us would accomplish anything in life without it. But the heroic will is often trumped by the depth, ubiquity, and energy of those intrusive ideas. Thus, most of us fail to diet sufficiently over a long enough period of time because our will is subverted by an inner urgency. Or we fail to begin what we believe we should do, or we fail to stop doing what has proved detrimental to ourselves or others. Clearly, heroic will can only make certain headway for us, which is why dieting centers and fad diets are so profitable for the owners and why Twelve Step groups are so ubiquitous. (By the way, I am very much in support of Twelve Step programs, as they have proved more efficacious than most alternatives through the last ninety years. For some, the addiction has moved from the substance to a group identification, a less damaging strategy for sure.)

If ever one is to triumph over an addiction, one is first summoned to feel more consciously what one has already been feeling, suffer what seems insufferable, and live through this experience without the reflexive management system. We never "solve" those unbidden ideas because they are an intimate part of our common human condition. We are born into perilous states and end by dying, so have a nice day! The question remains, however, to what degree our life is governed by these fears, and to what degree our management systems own us and manage us, and with what troubling consequences.

How many of us are able to bring the core fears and anxieties into consciousness, to see and acknowledge what they are truly about, and how many of us are able to go through *those* fears without the treatment plan we cobbled together?

Not only do addictions bring harmful consequences to our lives, they also narrow them as one gets obsessed about our obsessional treatment plans for our obsessions. These unbidden ideas are obsessions, for they impose themselves upon us and cause distress and compulsions, as we are driven to behaviors dedicated to their prospective amelioration. But our thoughts, behaviors, and lives get oriented around these intrusive ideas and, therefore, narrowed. As Jungian analyst Marion Woodman wrote, "Compulsions narrow life down until there is no living—existence perhaps, but no living."[1] In Greek mythology, Ixion is tied to a wheel that turns continuously in the underworld. Addictions oblige us to venture into our personal underworld wherein we experience the same old, same old, as noted by the character of Satan in *Paradise Lost*. As Gregory Bateson observed, the obsessional drinker believes he or she can challenge the "spirits." The game is on, and more often the "spirits" win, so the drinker is imprisoned by that which he first sought.

This hidden spiritual desire, this need for transcendent "connection," for "getting high," was identified in a letter exchange between Carl Jung and Bill W., who founded Alcoholics Anonymous. Jung suggested to Bill W. that Twelve Step programs acknowledge the profound role of our spiritual hunger, our spiritual thirst. Unless one can differentiate that quite legitimate, necessary motive from the substance upon which he or she has projected, one will remain its bewitched captive.

Asking ourselves questions like "What do I repeatedly do under stress?" or "What patterns do I find harmful but resistant to my efforts?" or perhaps even "What do I find objectionable in my life but am powerless to stop?" begins the forensic search for our addictive responses. Clearly, some of our reflexive response patterns are more harmful than others, particularly those where we risk the health of our bodies or may harm others. Others, like prayer and mantra, are less consequential, even "harmless," but can still keep us distanced from encountering what is troubling our souls. A less harmful response to life's disorders may be a step forward, and it may augur well for the prospect, but the time will come when we have to grow enough to take our life on, step into a larger space where the old protections are outgrown, and reclaim ownership of our lives.

Freeing oneself from one's addictive behaviors requires identifying what emotional reality or perception one is defending against through the addiction, and risk bearing what has been perceived as unbearable. Going through the fear rather than defending against it is the only way we can stop Ixion's wheel. There is no shame in fearing abandonment or suffering from boredom or depression. Until we can feel these things, really feel them and not anaesthetize them, we will remain unmotivated to change our lives.

Piercing the veil, deconstructing the mechanics of the addictive cycle, and identifying the primal, unassimilated idea for which our behaviors are a failing treatment plan is necessary. Then, as free persons, adults, we find we can in fact bear the unbearable, think the unthinkable, suffer the insufferable, and be free.

4

Active Imagination and the Encounter with the Daimon Within

In the next two chapters, I wish to review the tools we have to discern, differentiate, and decide anew in conducting this life: "active imagination" and "dream work."

W. B. Yeats once wrote that our dreams begin to identify our tasks and the responsibilities they ask of us. And when a young man in Vienna disowned the shocking content of one of his dreams, saying, "But I am not responsible for what my dreams say," Freud responded with "And who, then, do you think is?" So, at 4 am today I awoke, dreaming I was in some sort of adult education class and we had all been given a section of the surrounding blackboard to depict our "vision" of the universe. But how to depict this graphically? I wished I were a painter and could capture the images, but I am not, and words only left a trace of their passing. I thought of a story Robert Hansen told me of an ancient emperor who challenged the competing religions of his kingdom to depict their view of the universe. The Hindus portrayed an incredibly complex interaction of swirling bodies, some human, some gods, in an ancient dance of copulative arrivals and departures. The Buddhists took their brushes and swept the wall so clean that it shone, and when one looked at the wall, one saw oneself staring back.

As the dream unwound, I stewed over this assignment for forty-five minutes, eating up nearly half of the two hours we were allotted. Finally, I realized I had to take chalk to the board and begin before it was too late. When I arrived at my section of blackboard, the fellow in the section next to me had thoughtlessly allowed his composition to overrun my section so I only had about 40 percent of the space everyone else had. I was angry but thought I would just have to make do with what was available, what was left, and I began writing. And then I woke.

This was not the first time I had awakened with a "text" rolling out. Several articles and at least two books began this way. What are we to make of this phenomenon when some Other within is so busily creating and confronting our ego consciousness with such puzzling images? At the very least, I needed to consider where in my life I felt pressure to express myself or meet some sort of expectation, even while feeling crimped, constricted, and controlled by outer responsibilities and expectations.

It is clear that the psyche is polyvalent, having many, sometimes contradictory values, any one of which may be activated in a moment. I normally receive several dreams per day from clients. In most cases, I have to remind them that they actually do dream, and to pay attention, to record them, and to bring them to session the next time. In looking at my own dream, I realize that the thoughtless fellow who had usurped much of my space was a part of me. But what part? What came up was the overcommitted part, the part that tries to respond to all emails, that seeks to keep up on developments, and often crowds out what might be wishing to emerge into consciousness. The sheer busyness of life pushes aside the soul's quieter voice in the same way the dog pushes the cat aside to eat its food.

I recalled the dream "parable" of the two wall paintings. While quite different in their execution, each depicts a cosmic perspective, each embodying a grand tradition of piety and praxis and one of them reminding us of the summons to dive into the messiness of life, what Yeats called "the fury and the-mire of human veins."[1] The Other reminds us that all things emanate from within, and if we do not pay attention to the processes at work within ourselves, we are at the mercy of them. Our ego is a thin wafer afloat on an iridescent ocean populated by many scintillas of energy, sparkling creatures, cascading falls, and eruptions—all of them a part of us.

In my previous book, *The Broken Mirror: Refracted Images of Ourselves*, I explored the obstacles we face in learning what is going on within each of us. For example, there are basic attitudes that stand in the way of self-exploration: intimidation, skepticism, and lassitude. In seriatim fashion, intimidation by the magnitude of the universe within keeps us timorous and tentative; skepticism's doubts about our worth, legitimacy, and permission keep us from opening closed doors; and lassitude tells us it is all too much work and we should just take the rest of the day off. Additionally, the adaptations of childhood tend to become a reflexive internal operating system and our lives evolve mostly into stimulus-response adaptive behaviors that dictate our governing patterns. Further, our need for security and predictability requires us, from infancy onward, to "story" our environmental experiences and try to make sense of them with a narrative that may or may not accurately explain that formative moment, but years later imposes upon a new world the patterns and limitations of the old. Accordingly, we all tend to get locked into our adaptive and attitudinal responses and separate more and more from our soul's agenda for us.

Ego consciousness cannot handle all this traffic, so a good percentage of daily life is lived unconsciously, adaptively, or in service to agendas quite separated from deliberated choices. Other aspects of our psychic reality are split off or dissociated because they intimidate, or contradict, the conscious attitudes of the person. This material is "Shadow." The Shadow is not evil, per se, although it may include our capacity for evil; rather, it is all that is contradictory to our ego intentions and constructed sense of self, which is contrary to "what I wish to be and profess." Since no one is excluded from the full range of the human animal, our closet is full of agendas and capacities that we do not wish to do or be or stand for consciously. Thus, greed, lust, violence, avariciousness, and so on are always present and, when they are not being directly engaged by consciousness, have a tendency to range freely and act out on their own. So if we act in a harsh, unfair, even cruel way with another, we will have a ready "story" to justify our acts—if we even bother to reflect upon them.

Much human discord and suffering come out of the Shadow that acts with impunity and a large measure of autonomy. Living a thoughtful, accountable, "moral" life naturally requires a high degree of vigilance and self-inquiry and a willingness to accept, as the Roman comic dramatist Terence wrote over two millennia ago, that "nihil a me humanum alien puto," or "nothing human is alien to me." Understandably, Shadow work is difficult and always humbling, so we can see why it is so frequently neglected until the consequences of our behaviors force us to the table of accountability. Even there, our familiar friends, excuses, rationalizations, blame, and shabby evasions, are present to perpetuate the Shadow's disturbing presence in our lives. This dissociated material travels wherever we travel and remains a part of who we are, whether we recognize our disreputable cousins within or not.

One of the reasons depth psychologists work with dreams is because they bring up, sooner or later, these dissociated parts, these psychic presences, that are just as real, just as deserving of attention, as our most common conscious values and preferences. Candice Bergen would frequently find her father, the noted ventriloquist Edgar Bergen, in serious conversation with his wooden friend, Charlie McCarthy. When she asked him what he was doing talking to a dummy, her father replied that Charlie was so much wiser than he. In his own fashion, Mr. Bergen had stumbled upon the tool of active imagination, facilitating a dialogue that evoked aspects of himself and allowed those split-off dimensions of the soul to visit.

Over the entrance to his home in Zürich, Jung carved a phrase in Latin that, translated, reads, "Called or Not Called, God Is There." His citation of this ancient Greek aphorism is his reminder that there is an invisible world present that is always contiguous with the visible world. Just because we are unconscious of it doesn't mean it is not there moving and shaping us. The timeless debate over whether we are free or determined continues with the increasing preponderance of evidence suggesting that there are perhaps always invisible forces that shape our decisions. Still, Jean-Paul Sartre argued, free or determined, we must act "as if" we are free. That attitude brings to us opportunity and accountability, both necessary for any lived moral life.

The stakes are high in this matter; free or not, we are to act and be accountable as if we are free. The tool Jung evolved to facilitate this dialogue with the internal world is "active imagination." Our summons is to what the Swiss call an Auseinandersetzung, what we might call "dialogues," or "setting one thing over against another" in order to clarify the dynamic context in which all things occur. He was driven to develop the technique of active imagination to work with the turbulent images that flooded him after his break from Freud in 1912 and his entry into a midlife passage with no clear agenda. He dialogued with those images, recorded that conversation, and sometimes painted them in a magnificent volume now published as *The Red Book*. When I was a student in Switzerland in the 1970s, *The Red Book* had mythic status. We did not know for sure that it even existed, although there were rumors that a few of Jung's still-living contemporaries had seen it. Now published for the world to view, Jung's work with his own psyche is exemplary for its courage, its consistent discipline and attentiveness, and even its aesthetic achievement through his artwork and calligraphy.

In his memoir *Memories, Dreams, Reflections*, Jung describes his understandable apprehension of those depths he was exploring. But rather than run from them, he chose to engage them, learn their names, and ask of them their wisdom. Among those characters that emerged was one he called Philemon, an ancient presence who embodied the wisdom of the ages. As he met other characters, Jung confessed that at first it seemed like a defeat that so much was still unknown within him. It would only be a "defeat" if one clings to the ego phantasy of sovereignty and superiority. What Jung discovered was that it is the strong ego that handles this dialogue, holds its own, and yet is enlarged by the dialogue with the Other.

In my book on relationship, *The Eden Project*, I contend that the chief gift of relationship is not that the Other will fix or heal our brokenness but that the sharing of the otherness of the Other will enlarge us. Through internalizing the otherness of the Other, and still holding our conscious position, we grow. I have learned so much from my wife, for example, and perhaps she from me, and yet we retain our individuality and separate interests. When we think of such enlargements as a "defeat," it suggests how resistant the ego may be to change and challenge. (The contentious divisions in our nation presently stem from one elemental phenomenon: the resistance of the timorous ego of many to changes in definitions, categories, peoples, socio-economic structures, and so on. Since the nature of nature is change, change will always win out, even if it takes a century of persistence.)

What Jung tapped into is the mythopoetic nature of the human psyche. It repeatedly forms new images, new understandings, new marching orders. Of course, such change frequently challenges, or threatens, the old positions of the ego, and hence, we resist our internal conversations. As a result, the growth of the person stultifies and ultimately leads to some pathology, such as stuckness, depression, self-medication, and so on.

Active imagination, rather than stultification, leads to the dialectic and facilitates growth, just as dream work does. One of the advantages of active imagination is that it is not passive, as in waiting for a dream, but dynamic—namely, setting the dialogue in motion by addressing the Other within. Active imagination is not meditation, mindfulness, or guided imagery as are practiced in other circles. As the name suggests, it means "activating the image" that comes to us. So, for example, if one has a disturbing figure in a dream, rather than repress that quantum of energy elsewhere to do its damaging work, we engage it, ask why it has come and what it wants from us. From the perspective of conventional thinking, such a practice is "crazy" or navel-gazing. But given that such energy will not disappear but will rather go underground and pop up in some unexpected way, we choose to engage, to interrogate, to be open to learn something more about our intricate and complex selves.

Active imagination does not mean the loss of the ego's role in life decisions and accountability but instead requires the ego to be open to dialogue with the self, to respectfully attend a meeting of two layers of the psyche that rise from the meeting point of outer and inner worlds. The autonomous energies within us will, from time to time, adhere to an image, just as filings move toward the magnet. Active imagination is, then, attending to that image so it may be valued and clarified and, thereby, become instructive to us. Only when adhering to an image can the unconscious become conscious. We respect that image and its autonomy, but we do not relinquish the ego's hold on daily reality because we are always called back to the tasks of daily life. Yet this internal dialogue enlarges and informs the capacity of consciousness to deal with the demands of the hour.

When we dialogue with an image, we are investigating an incarnation of the invisible, intangible world. Often attributed to Surrealist poet Paul Éluard, a contemporary of Jung, the phrase "There is another world, and it is in this one"[2] is apt in this regard. For example, one focuses on a puzzling, unfinished dream or a dream figure that seems troubling, and one permits those images freedom and spontaneity without losing the frame of reference of the ego. We may track that dialogue by writing it down, painting it, sculpting it, or dancing it. Any means is useful providing it has plasticity and can temporarily hold the energy of the image. The purpose is not to empty the ego world but to enlarge it by bringing more to the table for conversation.

Understandably, we have certain internal resistances to this process. First, we need to find, perhaps seize, permission. Most of us do not feel we have permission to own our lives, and this work is sure to rouse that self-doubt. A second problem is skepticism, whereby we say this is just something we are "making up." In his book *Inner Work*, Robert Johnson wrote of a client who was resistant to treatment and confessed that the "dreams" he brought into therapy were all made up. But Johnson noted that the material he brought in was in fact descriptive of the client's struggles. In other words, the client had probably backed into the technique of active imagination as he probed his psyche in "making up" the dream content. What emerged, no surprise, was in fact the very material that had brought him to therapy in the first place. The third resistant point is generated by fear. After all, we have worked hard to attain a conscious point of reference with whatever security fences we wish to erect around it. Why would we wish to undo it? However logical that resistance, it is also what leads to the stuckness of the soul, a stuckness that sooner or later will pathologize as nature's protest of our rigidity.

Jung observed that if we went into a forest and encountered strange animals and plant life, we would not think we had created those entities. So it is, he argued, that the intrapsychic aspects of our unconscious are just as real. While the ego needs to hold its position, it can also be expanded by the dialogue that evolves out of this respect for the autonomous other.

> If the psyche tells you what you think
> you already know, then you don't know
> it well enough, or as well as you think.

Approaching these intrapsychic parts of ourselves is best facilitated by creating a personal ritual whereby one removes as many distractions as possible and settles into one's body. We note the many distractions and how hard it sometimes is to focus. Each of us may find a different medium, but most folks use a pad and pen with the intent to record as much as possible without interrupting or dominating the flow of imagery. If, for example, you are seeking to question a figure in your dream, keep returning to that image. Ignore the skeptical voice within that says you are only "making it up." As with any practice, the more you do this, the easier it may become. Treat that dream image with respect, write it down, talk to it, and listen to it.

Sometimes folks will utilize paints, colored pens, clay, and bodily movement; however, active imagination is not an exercise in fine arts. The more "primitive" and spontaneous, the better. While our Auseinandersetzung with the image may sometimes attain an aesthetic dimension, this is not about art; it is about embodying the psychic energy to make it available to consciousness. The problem with the unconscious is that it is unconscious, so we need to work with those processes—dreams, somatic exercises, active imagination—that help incarnate the invisible world and render it approachable.

Whatever emerges from this process is to be approached with the same methodology as working with dreams. Listen to the image and amplify its possible associations and cultural references in the context of your contemporary life. Who are these figures? What is the time and place? What are the effects generated by the images? Is there a plot line? Remember, as with dreams, some images resist "interpretation." Leave them that way, and the symbolic material will continue to percolate through your psyche and often send up recurrent waves of associations and insights.

One caveat to remember: use active imagination only with intrapsychic images and not with living persons. We are force fields of energy, and changing the dynamics with another can easily fall into power issues or alter the field between you and the other person, and not necessarily in a beneficent way. Ultimately, the purpose of active imagination is to gain knowledge of one's own soul, and the purpose ultimately of knowledge is action. One must take this conversation with the soul with such gravity and serious intent that one is obliged to change one's life as a result. In seeing, we are, as Rilke noted in "The Archaic Torso of Apollo," seen as well: "For there is no place that does not see you. . . . You must change your life."[3]

Going back to my dream of the blackboard, I reentered the setting and immediately felt stress and anxiety in my body. A competitive atmosphere is common to people's dreams—the exam for which one is not prepared, the return to the university to fulfill more credits—so one has to inquire: Where am I feeling challenged? Where am I under pressure? Is there any specific locus, or is it generic? When I approached the fellow who was thoughtlessly spilling over into my space and time, I found him full of excuses and rationalizations for getting lost amid the thousands of distractions and interruptions of modern life, red herrings to which we all succumb and thereby lose the thread of our developmental journey. When I encountered his recalcitrance, I knew it called for more intentionality on my part, including setting aside two times, early morning and evening, to address all the emails and other requests I had received. I was aware of this tension, this abiding frustration in my life, but when I engaged that intrapsychic Other within me, it all became more tangible, more clearly requiring action and commitment.

So many times the ego is tempted to conclude, "Oh, I know about that issue. That's all this means." But if the psyche makes the effort to embody the issue in the dream, to underline its perspective that too many distractions are inimical to psychic health, then it is time to take the matter seriously. If the psyche tells you what you think you already know, then you don't know it well enough, or as well as you think. And whatever emerges from this prospect is considered important by the Daimon within each of us, the guiding spirit that links us to the transpersonal.

Over time, the utilization of active imagination moves one from a passive posture, waiting for dreams to show up, to an active engagement with the soul. Ultimately, this tool is instrumental in our recovery of personal authority. If I take seriously what emerges from the Auseinandersetzung, then I am operating from both a wider and a deeper framing of my life's journey. While our ego converses with the transient cacophonies of popular culture and its distractions, the soul traverses timeless zones, transpersonal frames in which our personal journeys take on greater depth, dignity, and gravitas. We move to rhythms that are far greater in their amplitude than the preoccupations of daily life and its noisy demands. We live lives that are ours, yes, but they also belong to more than us. Active imagination is a practical tool for each of us to move from passivity to engagement with the psyche that is seeking to connect to us, to heal us, and to enlarge us.

Remembering speechlessly we seek the great forgotten language, the lost lane-end into heaven, a stone, a leaf, an unfound door. Where? When? O lost, and by the wind grieved, ghost, come back again.

—Thomas Wolfe

5

Spectral Visitants

Still another resource nature provides us occurs each night through the spectral visitation of dreams, and psychoanalysis has provided the tool to open the hidden treasure that the unconscious brings. All of us are curious about our dreams, but so few are curious enough to work with them over time and enter a dialogue with them. As an analyst, I have, as other analysts have, worked with thousands of dreams over the last half-century. As a result, I am less intimidated by the process and more accustomed to the patient questioning and probing that this work demands. When folks say, "You're not going to believe this dream," I think, "Yes, I am. I have probably seen a version of it heretofore, and many times."

As an old German proverb has it, "Träume sind Schäume"— literally, "Dreams are froth"—they are only worthless firings of neurons at the end of a long day. And yet, if we live to be eighty, we will have spent six years of our life in this reportedly worthless activity. But does it make sense to conclude that nature wastes energy, that all that concentrated activity is devoid of purpose? The ancients and Indigenous tribes still conclude that their dreams were the means by which the gods spoke through them. While traveling in Africa, Jung found that several of the peoples he visited made a distinction between big dreams and small dreams. The latter were important but only to the individual. The former were meant to be shared with the elders of the tribe to obtain the wisdom imparted by the celestial powers.

What are we to make of these spectral visitants that come to us an average of six times per sleep cycle? So often the images of dreams may seem frightening or, the reverse, are fantastical enough to send the ego off in a denial of their importance. But I believe, and so do my colleagues, that there is no such thing as a "bad" dream. One may experience frightening images or the dream may raise troubling issues, but the psyche's intent is to bring matters to the surface in order for us to deal with them. Ignoring the thrust of the dream merely means that whatever issues are at work will continue to go about their business in the unconscious. Ignoring issues does not mean they will go away; it means they will work with greater intensity to win our attention to them. As Freud once wryly noted, we may deny their messages by day but live them at night.

Part of the difficulty in interpreting our own dreams is that we tend to literalize the images and get stuck in the thicket of their opacity, or we are put off by their seeming threats. If we recall that the dream comes embodied in a tissue of metaphor, then we have to ask what issues are analogously evoked in order to understand what is really going on in our psyche. If, for example, one feels a sense of shame or embarrassment or one finds oneself lost in a strange place within a dream, then one has to ask what issues in one's contemporary life trigger such reactions. The twin agendas of the psyche—seeking the fullest possible expression in life's arena and self-healing—are at work in those moments. While ego consciousness would prefer other topics, the psyche is saying that the issue that generated the dream has a quantum of energy that cries out for redress, or at least acknowledgement. In the paragraphs that follow, I hope to lay out a few basic understandings, approaches to dreams, and methods that one may use in working with one's dreams.

First, we need to remember the difference between signs and symbols. Both utilize images, but the former image points to a known content just as a road sign advises us to stop or yield. A sign has an identifiable content or "message." A symbol, however, is an image that points in the direction of, or intimates, something that might otherwise be inexplicable, such as a feeling state or a moral dilemma. Secondly, we need to always think in terms of analogy; namely, what is a parallel life situation that may be evoked by the dream's imagery. If one dreams of a peculiar act, for example, one has to not reject the dream because of that peculiarity but rather ask what life circumstances might one recall in which that feeling state or situation is analogized. Thirdly, the personal associations of the dreamer are critical. If you dream of your grandmother, it may stir associations with my grandmother, but they were different grandmothers and are internalized by each of us in our unique and idiosyncratic ways. It is easy for the listener to fill in the blanks with her or his associations, but it is the dreamer's dream, and the dreamer's associations, that drive our approach to interpretation.

There are different types, or categories, of dreams. Many dreams are "reactive," or "processing," dreams, that is, dreams that are triggered by the stimuli and debris of daily life. Too often, then, the ego says, "I know what that dream means! X happened at work yesterday, and that is what triggered this dream." We think by identifying a trigger we have explained the dream. First of all, the psyche has no obligation to respond to the detritus of daily life unless it so chooses for its own purposes, and secondly, it may be that the psyche is not commenting on the event but, analogously, reacting to a situation, an evocation of a mood, for example, that the situation catalyzed. At the very least, the "processing" or "reactive" dream indicates there is more energy circulating around the issues than one may have known otherwise.

Secondly, there are "compensatory" dreams, that is, dreams that embody the psyche's effort to bring neglected values to bear on the one-sidedness of our lives. If, for example, the dreamer maintains an intellectual distancing from the difficulties the dream evokes, then one may have to recognize the amount of affect that has been pushed aside. Or one finds that corrective elements enter the mix, seeking balance in one's psychic life that has been denied by the pressures and the thousand adaptations to the stresses of daily life. For example, a female client of mine, who was struggling with settling her deceased parents' estate and updating the house inherited from them, dreamt that there was a jam in the kitchen sink that kept the water from flowing and threatened to flood the house. At the same time in the dream, there was a plumber figure in the basement who was going to open the jam and allow things to flow smoothly again. When we explored her associations with that plumber character, a path of action emerged for her to follow and, in so doing, to move through and beyond the emotional congestion her overwhelming feelings had played in her inertia. While the death of parents is always eventful in a person's life, this dreamer had been too close to her parents, and they too controlling of her. Thus, when they passed on, she was unprepared for the assumption of responsibility for selling or rehabilitating their house, or for electing the course of her new life. Her psychic energy was so captivated by the parent/child imago that she felt paralyzed. And yet her psyche announced to us an energy existed in her underground, and an ongoing trust in and dialogue with that figure would, and did, bring her own adult capacities into play so her life might move on to a larger journey. She was no longer her parents' daughter; she was a grown woman with her life to live.

Thirdly, there are "archetypal" dreams, that is, dreams that may have a topical link, but which draw from the deep thesaurus of imagery in the psychic inheritance of humankind. This is the "big dream" that Indigenous populations came to respect so highly. The dream is both personal and transpersonal at the same time. Dreams of journeys, descents and ascents, death and rebirth, and so on are typical sources of archetypal imagery. Any of us can literally have the same dream tonight as was dreamt by others in other times and places, for we all carry within the same symbol-making capacity as those who went before us.

Fourthly, there are "precognitive" or "prophetic" dreams. They are rare, but they exist and have been reported from the earliest times up through the present. Somehow, the dreamer's psyche has trolled the depths of the hour and formed some impressions of what is going on elsewhere or what has not yet happened in the tangible world. The prophetic vision of Emanuel Swedenborg is an example. He was flooded with imagery of a fire happening in Stockholm while he was in Gothenburg. Subsequently, reports arrived that at that exact time a fire had consumed that part of Stockholm of which he had dreamed. Who can understand those dreams, and yet they are just as real. I had a client who had more than one prophetic dream. It seemed that she was "wired" to some sort of energy coursing beneath the surface of daily life. Her psychic membrane was so permeable that she picked up on clues that lay far beneath the surface of daily life.

Additionally, any dream can have objective and subjective readings. The objective level may literally be commenting on how a relationship is faring, or not faring, but the subjective level of interpretation asks us to see that the various figures and features of the dream are also aspects of the dreamer. So it is problematic to discern, if I dream of my child for example, whether I am processing something to do with that relationship or the psyche is borrowing the child to embody some aspect of my own inner child. This is why it's often efficacious to start with the objective approach to the dream to see if the unconscious is casting light on the time and tides of daily life and then look at the images as intrapsychic aspects of the dreamer. In the end, one must consider both objective and subjective readings of the dream for a fuller approach to understanding it.

Jung identified four stages of the analytic work with dreams: confession, interpretation/elucidation, reeducation, and transformation. We all know there is something inherently healing in telling one's story, being heard, and feeling held in a nonjudgmental way. Merely getting it off one's chest can be a powerful experience even without interpretation (more on this soon). "Reeducation," or "Nacherzieung," as Freud called it, involves exploring the range of alternative choices one may attempt, remembering that many times the hole we have dug ourselves into has been reinforced many, many times, so reeducation takes time. Only in the movies does one have a sudden revelatory insight and everything falls into place. "The butler did it," and the mystery is solved. In real life, the person will have to practice new attitudes and behaviors repeatedly for change to occur. Lastly, over time, the powerful merging of insight and changed behaviors produces an enlarged personality structure. As Jung pointed out, we seldom "solve" these lifelong patterns, but we can outgrow them and lead a more satisfying and productive life.

> Working with one's dreams over time is the shifting of authority in the dreamer's life from their environmental pressures to their inner life from whence their deepest truths emerge.

Every dream, just as every short story, has an elemental structure, usually involving one or more entities of the dreamer's "life-situation," such as act, scene, agent, time, and place. It is a natural error on our part to focus too much on the plot line of the dream. The story may be important, of course, but it can also distract from another constituent element that is just as significant.

One notes these structural elements as part of the targeting and shaping of the dream's import. So if the scene dominates—for example, a childhood home or school—then one can say either that the dream is exploring unfinished business from that stage of one's journey or, more commonly, something in the present has activated that history as a metaphoric linkage of past and present. I had a client with a puzzling dream from early schooling, and only as she was walking out the door did she remember a particular incident with a particular child, and her acute humiliation that followed. We realized that what she was processing was a contemporary experience of embarrassment. We both marveled at the psyche's wisdom in storing away that long-deposited memory and its resurrection at this much later date to help her probe the damage a more recent experience had exacted from her.

Similarly, the agents may be anonymous figures, contemporaries, or children from long ago and far away, but what brings them together today? I had one analysand for whom about 50 percent of his dreams had to do with his parents' house, their bedroom, or the street on which they lived. As one might surmise, he was struggling still to gain greater purchase on his often shaky adulthood, given how influenced he remained by the parental dynamics.

To use a non-dream example, Samuel Beckett's classic play *Waiting for Godot* has two Laurel and Hardy–type characters who sit around and gab for two hours. Their landscape is arid and nondescript, the time is irrelevant, and the action is non-action. (Both acts end by a character saying, "Let's go," but the stage direction dictates, "They do not move.") In fact, there is nowhere for them to go and nothing for them to do because Beckett's play is a portrait of a state of being, the post–World War II condition of traumatized silence, with no act that either restores the old road map or finds a newer one.

After noting the Sitz im Leben, or the "setting in life" of the dream, we gather the associations for the characters, events, locale, and so forth. Then we look to other cultural associations that may be applicable to the dream and identify any archetypal motifs that may be present. So a dreamer might dream of a pop star and get caught in whether or not she or he likes that person's music, but in the dream it was the content of the lyric being sung that was called upon by the dream-maker.

In general, the more associations we can put out on the table, the better, but the key is the feeling response any particular image triggers in the dreamer. Sometimes the dreamer is too close to the imagery to see anything there, but more often it is the dreamer's emotional assent that tells us we are tracking the dream as it might wish. Dream dictionaries are of limited use, as they tend to make too many literal associations and then claim "This is what the dream image means." Again, your grandmother is not my grandmother, so we have to be a bit more agnostic in our approach to the dream and more open to its promptings.

Many years ago, when I was in my first full-time teaching position in academia, a colleague brought me a dream, not because I was known for interpreting dreams but because I played a role in his dream. In the dream, at a critical moment, I, having heard his dilemma, ritualistically took a strip of masking tape and placed it on the end of his nose. In the dream, and as he brought me the dream, he knew I would not have performed that bizarre act without it meaning something.

"Well, Bob," I blurted out, more lucky than knowing, "what you are looking for is as near as the end of your nose." This simplistic statement was in fact quite telling, as Bob was facing a major challenge in determining his future life course. What he needed to know—and in part already knew—was as near as the end of his nose. Usually, the unconscious knows so much more than we consciously know, and I remain humbled by this natural but recondite wisdom we all carry within.

When, in 1900, Freud published *Die Traumdeutung*, the meaning of, or interpretations of dreams, he was writing for fellow physicians. Though it is now considered a seminal work, it sold fewer than five hundred copies at the time of publication. Anyone who claims they can, with confidence, tell you what a dream means is blowing smoke in your ear (even Freud). Dream work is work, and it is a very uncertain forensic endeavor. It is more art than science and method. There is no final interpretation. As poets say, a poem is never finished; it is only abandoned. So it is with dream work.

One of the secondary effects of working with one's dreams over time is the shifting of authority in the dreamer's life from their environmental pressures to their inner life from whence their deepest truths emerge. Also, over time, one begins to underline and watch for recurrent motifs in the dream imagery. There is a personal iconography for all of us, and when one pays attention, one starts to recognize the recurrence of those motifs.

Let me share a couple of my favorite client dreams. I call them favorites because, even though I received them decades ago, I knew upon first hearing them that I would not forget them, and I marveled then, as I do now, at the ingenuity of the unconscious to produce such elaborate narratives and imagery. Before telling you these dreams, let me say, yes, you may tell me you don't dream in as much detail as these examples, but in fact you do, if you remember enough and write them down and study them. The more one is committed to working with dreams, the more we tend to remember them and are able to commit them to a written summary. No one knows what happens in the unconscious, by definition, but as dreams are remembered we have a meeting point where the product of the unconscious and the recording consciousness touch and enlarge each other. Jung described this activity as "the transcendent function," namely, the activity of the psyche to transcend the conscious/unconscious boundaries and the space in between. Symptoms are one example of this function, and dreams are another. Both allow us to approach the unknowable through the limited purview of the knowable and to see how these two worlds interact and amplify each other. We may not know what is transpiring in the unconscious, but by attending the meeting point of these two realms, the dream, we may get a large clue.

Both of these dreamers were German women and I met both while still in training in Zürich. The first dreamer was a sixty-five-year-old woman who had lost her husband. She had grown up in a patriarchal family and her father was her hero, mentor, and guide in all things. She had only married in her forties, when her father was dying. Now her husband, who had been half a generation older than she, had died. At first our work was, appropriately, focused on her grieving. After my prodding her to remember her dreams, she finally recalled a dream, and it set the tone for the rest of our work.

In the dream she was on a pilgrimage of some kind with "Otto," her husband. They walked through a flower-strewn garden until they reached a flowing stream with a stone archway over it. As they started across the stream, she realized she had forgotten her purse and needed to go back to her parked car to fetch it. She did, and retraced her steps to catch up with Otto. As she reached the stone arch, she was joined by a man who she felt was familiar and yet unknown to her. Uncharacteristically, she told this stranger her capsulated life story, up to and including her recent bereavement. She concluded her narrative with the sentence "I've been so alone; I've been so alone." He replied, "I know, and it has been good for me," pointing to himself. Both in the dream, and in her retelling of it to me, she was offended by his seeming insensitivity to her loss.

Inwardly, I rejoiced at this dream because it was perhaps the first time in her life since early childhood that she had looked within for directions instead of following the well-meant external authorities that had governed her life. That dream signaled our transition from a reactive grieving process to a developmental agenda, as well as her entrée to the larger agenda of the second half of life—the recovery of personal authority. The known/unknown man was, of course, a part of her, what Jung called the animus, or the inner masculine energy of the woman that enables her to take her desires and values into the world. When the bridge to the outer world is missing, she will live a life of deferred authority and a short-changing of her unique offerings. It took the death of both father and husband, and for the smoke to clear, for her to meet this missing component of her developmental agenda. While she had had a distinguished professional career, the same as her scientific father, she had always lived her life on his playing field. As the stranger announced, it took her suffering, and the removal of the external authorities, for her to begin to find her own.

Our work deepened and her journey became more and more her life to live rather than satisfying the plans of others. Such motifs as "journey," "crossing over," "bridging," and so on illustrate the life-setting in which she is invited to become her own person. She had left her purse behind—the receptacle and carrier of her identity, papers, credit cards, keys, and *instrumentalities*—and it had to be recovered before her journey could resume. The stranger had been there all along, but he was essentially unknown to her, for the external instructions she followed were benign, formative, and well-intended. Only the trauma of death could pry loose that stranger from his intrapsychic slumber so he could become a greater part of her thoughtful, considered life.

The second dream was from a translator and teacher of foreign languages. She had lost both parents as a result of the war and had grown up under the harsh tutelage of her mother's sister, who made it clear that she wanted nothing to do with her. As a child, she got into petty theft and an addiction to chocolate. Can we blame a child for looking for some toy, some delight, some sweetness to enter her life, even if she had to steal it? Later, as an adult, she avoided going to university and translated and taught languages to individuals and small groups because she could remain more or less in control of her environment.

When she brought the following dream, I was astonished because of its obvious parallels with the motifs of fairy tales and its zeroing in on her defenses, avoidances, and challenges. In the dream, she was in a room holding a doll, a doll she knew, even in the dream, was her lost childhood. A witch entered the room and stole her doll. She pursued the witch and offered payment for its return, but the witch mocked her and ran on. She followed frantically. This time the witch said she would return the doll when the following ransom was paid: first, she must make love with a fat man; secondly, she must go to the university and give a public lecture; and thirdly, she must return to Germany to have a meal with her fractious aunt. She dissolved in tears as she knew that, symbolically, this was the price of healing, but her fears still stood so daunting.

What, we ask, is a witch doing in contemporary Switzerland? Well, the witch is the archetypal image associated with the dark side of the Great Mother archetype, the archetype of life and death itself. The dreamer had been exposed to death, destruction, and loss in an overwhelming way and, as we all do, became a prisoner over time to her defenses against this trauma. The stolen "doll" is, of course, what happened to her, along with many other children in that war-torn nation. She understood in the dream, and in our conversations, that the three tasks were symbolic expressions of facing her fears and laying claim to a larger life. Making love with a fat man was not only accepting an adult's embrace of sexuality but also embodied her fear of the anarchy of the body, an autonomy she "managed" through an eating disorder and her abstemious lifestyle. Giving a lecture at the university would demand that she both overcome her mild agoraphobia and lay claim to her intellectual gifts, which were considerable. And lastly, she was summoned to diminish the archetypal witch's powers by confronting and dining with the biographical witch's animosity toward her. In all three tasks, she was asked to grow up. Indeed, both dreamers were being asked by their unconscious to grow up and step into their true adult capacities. In each dream, we see both the restorative and developmental agendas of the human psyche at work.

Again, the reader may claim, "But I don't have such interesting dreams as these." That is exactly what both of these dreamers believed before they undertook the Auseinandersetzung, the dialectical give and take of the conscious/unconscious dynamic at work in all of us. What they found for themselves through their dream life was both a deeper personal authority and a much richer, more interesting life than when they were living, as we all do from time to time, reactively rather than generatively.

I invite you to start paying more attention to this vast theatre of engagement with the soul that transpires every night in each of us. Write the dream down before it escapes, and then take apart its images one by one, and you will find to your amazement that we all carry this rich, corrective, directive, and inviting source of wisdom inside.

Our ancestors rightly understood the message of the dreams as originating from powers transcendent to the purview and capacities of ordinary ego conscious life. Whether we use the metaphor of "the gods" or "the Self," we engage the transpersonal mysteries when we pay attention to the psychodrama that rises from miasmic depths each night as we sleep. If an invitation is being extended by those depths each night, who are we to run from this meeting with our own souls? Such a flight means we will be in service to the merely reactive, to the topical rather than the timeless, and to the loudest noise of the hour rather than the deeply echoing voice that tells us who we really are and for what we are really intended.

"Liquid modernity" is the growing conviction that change is the only permanence, and uncertainty the only certainty. A hundred years ago "to be modern" meant to chase "the final state of perfection"—now it means an infinity of improvement, with no "final state" in sight and none desired.

—Zygmunt Bauman

It's hard to confront senseless tragedy. It's easier to invent a story, and feel command over chaos, even if it amounts to a con.

—Dana Vachon

6

Divided Soul/Divided Nation

Reflections on the American Electorate

Throughout the pandemic, therapists worldwide reported increased anxiety, depression, and self-medication in their patients. Similarly, therapists in America have, over the past decade, reported a higher level of the same symptoms unrelated to COVID-19. Our general atmosphere of malaise, bitterness, and confrontation, not to mention the outbreaks of violence, have traumatized a nation. What we see on television, what we experience in our cities, and what we suffer in our disillusionment of a once semi-stable world naturally affects each of us and triggers not only our meta-complexes but our omnipresent anxieties and their defenses. This chapter, while seemingly diverging from our analytic and personal processes, acknowledges that we are all, also, citizens of the Polis, and that what happens in the collective experience reaches each of us, touches each of us, and triggers our deepest fears and our defenses against them.

There is a general warning for polite company, namely, never discuss politics and religion if you wish a civil and pleasant evening. Generally, I have adhered to that good advice. Still, for some years now, I and other therapists have been dealing with this enhanced patient anxiety and depression around the state of our country. Quite obviously, what happens around us affects and shows up in our personal lives. My hope for a civil, respectful discussion of what drives us, what divides us, and what unites us is up for grabs in this chapter. Reportedly, the great nineteenth-century physician Louis Pasteur kept a reminder of this on the lintel to his consulting room that I paraphrase as "Tell me not your politics and your religion. Tell me only your suffering."[1] It is in that spirit that I write these sentences.

My discussion here is less political than psychological, but we are all "politicians," given that we live in and contribute to the Polis. We were all "politicians" before we became partisans.

In addition to an increase in anxiety and depression, therapists across the country have reported that they have witnessed in their patients generalized perseveration on national circumstances for the last few years, greater sleep disturbances, and gastric and other somatic disorders. While initial reactions were stupor and denial, they have been replaced, generally, with anxiety and anger—the typical sequence of reactions to real or perceived threats to one's well-being. We have to recognize this fact and deal with it, remembering always the caution of Marcus Aurelius, who is usually credited with saying that everything we hear is an opinion, not a fact, and a perspective, not the "truth." Where there are no, or few, objective truths, there are always subjective experiences, not to mention complexes triggered. If the French philosopher Joseph de Maistre was right and "every nation gets the government it deserves," then recent history is showing us something about our personal and collective psyches.[2]

In 1929 H. L. Mencken wrote in the *Baltimore Sun*, "As democracy is perfected, the office of the President represents, more and more closely, the inner soul of the people. On some great and glorious day, the plain folks of the land will reach their heart's desire at last, and the White House will be occupied by a downright moron."[3]

So who are the people? In a letter to the *New Yorker* on December 5, 2016, a reader by the name of Yasmin Askari from Maryland wrote of those who voted for Donald Trump: "[They] are not the underbelly of America—they are simply America. The same America whose structural racism allowed the Supreme Court to strike down a key part of the Voting Rights Act and disproportionately disenfranchised minorities. The same America that allows the Executive Branch to perform extra-judicial killings of Muslims overseas. The same America that protests acts of hate on social media but stands by silently when a girl or a woman in hijab is harassed on the streets. This is not *all* of America, but it *is* America."

Even in this era of general well-being, we know there is a widening educational gap in our country, a wealth gap, an imaginative gap for a better future, and thus a breeding ground for anxiety, despair, anger, and protest.

Not so long ago an American politician said,

> Here is the challenge to our democracy: In this nation I see tens of millions of its citizens—a substantial part of its whole population—who at this very moment are denied the greater part of what the very lowest standards of today call the necessities of life. I see millions of families trying to live on incomes so meager that the pall of family disaster hangs over them day by day. I see millions whose daily lives in city and on farm continue under conditions labeled indecent by a so-called polite society half a century ago. I see millions denied education, recreation, and the opportunity to better their lot and the lot of their children. I see millions lacking the means

to buy the products of farm and factory and by their poverty denying work and productiveness to many other millions. I see one-third of a nation ill-housed, ill-clad, ill-nourished.

The speaker was Franklin Delano Roosevelt in 1937, in his Second Inaugural Address.

While the general economic state of the nation has improved over that Depression era, his words are both chilling and prophetic. One of Trump's voters said he voted for Trump because it is the only way people will notice he is here. Another said that they are the people you fly over when you go coast to coast. In his book *Hillbilly Elegy*, J. D. Vance wrote that the poor, left-behind whites are the most pessimistic group in America, even behind poor Black and Latino communities.

Who are "these people"? I grew up as one of them. My father was pulled out of eighth grade and sent to work in a factory for the rest of his life because of the Great Depression. My mother, an orphan, grew up in poverty and was a secretary. Their core message to me as a child, both overtly spoken and implicit, always was "Don't hope, don't expect, don't even ask, and that way you won't have your heart broken," as theirs had been throughout their lives. And they meant well by that admonition. They were trying to protect me, even as they gave me a message of passivity and resignation as marching orders. I am so deeply grateful that I grew up in a moment and context in history where a poor child could get an education and I was able to go to college. My lifelong Black friend across the street, the late, great Kent Wilson, even won a scholarship to Harvard. He went on to get an MBA and lived a full life in Baden bei Wien outside Vienna. In childhood, he lived on slices of bread with milk poured on them. No complaints, no grievances, nothing. We had no expectations, even as something in us pushed us to move away and travel to the dark side of the moon if necessary.

So what happened in 2016? The dispossessed spoke, the angry spoke, and while they were not the majority, they were enough to win through the archaic electoral system we have inherited from eighteenth-century politicians who designed a system to protect the nation lest the people rise up and elect the demagogue H. L. Mencken feared. Since that time, Trump has catalyzed, fed, and profited from the deep distress felt by so many of our compatriots, and now we are a nation divided and polarized. Back in the nineteenth century, Benjamin Disraeli, who went on to become prime minister of the United Kingdom, wrote of the two nations that contended in his time: the rich and the poor. This same widening gap threatens the stable order of the world itself as the gulf grows ever wider.

An even greater gap exists in our country between those who have hope for their futures and those who feel the future is moving on without them. For many religious conservatives, the demographics are against them. They become a smaller and smaller percentage of the body politic, and the values they consider essential are eclipsed by differing lifestyles and definitions. My parents believed that such matters as gender identity and gender roles were fixed by nature and divinity rather than social constructs that could be deconstructed as has repeatedly happened since. Races and ethnic groups presumably knew their place, and their place was clearly subservient. The world of "certainties," or "fixities," has dissolved and opened a vast gulf of ambiguity. The human ego does not like ambiguity; it prefers certainty and plans on a measure of control. As those "fixities" erode, the anxiety level rises, and hence the furor and frenzy of conservative groups over their loss of power and status.

Since the demographic curve is not on their side, many have sought to tinker with the system to retain power and looked for a "savior" to lead the charge against the postmodern world. In the face of uncertain headwinds, many long for the restoration of the old worldview. If it did not privilege them, and often it did, it reassured them. But, as we know, the nature of nature is change, and the changes roll onward no matter the counter-measures. Rolling back changes temporarily is not impossible, but in this case, the genie is out of the bottle and will not return to the old glass prison. As the late Polish sociologist and philosopher Zygmunt Bauman concluded, we live, as we have perhaps always lived, in a liquid world, not a static world. If modernity and postmodernity are defined by their liquidity, our clinging to the old is an exercise in futility. And desiring to live as one believes one used to live is delusional.

While much of the public is cynically distracted by so-called wedge issues, such as abortion, school prayer, and minority rights, the changes in our country are moving us toward the idea of liberty and justice for all, just as promised over two centuries ago. While there are bigots and racists in these voting groups, the vast majority are simply scared of the future and believe they do not have a role to play in it. By far the largest group are those who feel left behind by the times they knew: shifting economics and prospects for the future, loss of certainties, pressures from ethnic groups, computers, automation, and the migration of manufacturing centers. When I was a child, a common saying was "As GM goes, so goes the nation." That saying sounds rather quaint in light of Toyota, Mercedes, BMW, and the international economic transformations that have dominated the last few decades. Iconic US Steel is now a Japanese company, and most of our manufactured goods come from distant ports of call.

The cynical activation of these so-called wedge issues produce a great psychological conundrum; specifically, why would so many people vote against their interests? If, as the old political saying has it, "it's the economy, stupid," then why do so many, with the chief industries already fled to foreign shores, or exhausting their resources as coal and gas have, vote for candidates who are economically in servitude to those fading industries? The answers to that conundrum are complex, to be sure, but the bottom line is fear. Fear of change, fear of ambiguity, fear of loss of understanding and control. For any of us, substantive and rapid change will produce these atavistic and protective reactions, but some can recover perspective and see the larger picture, and others cannot.

Study after study indicates people choose from their gut, not their heads, which means they choose from whatever complex is operative at the moment and thus are very hard to argue off of that static position. It is the creeping specter of change, with its attendant loss of certainties, that is the catalyst. Hence, the slogan "Make America Great Again" is a direct appeal to the phantasy that one can return to a simpler time, with simpler structures of belief and definition. The computer era, the imminence of artificial intelligence, the globalization of resources and values, and a growing emphasis on cultural diversity cause many to believe that the future does not include them. Thus, there is a nostalgia for a world that does not exist anymore and was not that great to start with (I do know this; I was there). It was an era that privileged a few and exploited many, where women and people of color suffered the squelching of their souls, and where honest questions and differing responses were not welcome. Such a world will only appeal to someone closed off and defended against change and not open to the world that has already become.

As an example of those voting against their apparent interests, evangelicals enthusiastically voted for a man who routinely violates their most cherished values. Jung recognized this tendency long ago: "People who merely believe and don't think continually expose themselves to their own worst enemy: *doubt.* Wherever belief reigns, doubt lurks in the background."[4]

Enthusiastically, they vote for a man who demeans women in general, and in particular, ridicules a Muslim couple who lost their son fighting for this country, mimics a journalist with a physical disability, makes lewd suggestions about his daughter, mimics his successor's history of stuttering, crudely hawks his shoddy products from education to Bibles, and invites Russia to interfere in our elections. He brags about paying no taxes, refuses to share his IRS returns, and spends his flock's hard-earned contributions on his many legal defenses. All of this, of course, is without any shame on his part. Shame would imply having a conscience. If one votes for and contributes money to someone whose behaviors flout one's deepest religious values, then something else is afoot. It's all not about what it's about. Only fear can account for such a reflexive blindness and moral contradiction.

A quick review of history reveals that when fear prevails, people may fall for anyone who will offer them surcease, amelioration, and restoration of the status quo ante. There *are* huge changes in our demography, huge changes in the international economy, huge changes in our economic profile. Uneducated white workers have reason to have concern as their jobs are cynically shipped overseas by boards that have no motive other than profit. So many look to a self-proclaimed strong man who can deliver them, even as he is our first president to have never held elective office heretofore, has no military experience, and thinks of nuclear weapons as something to take lightly. Such a figure, then, is less a savior than a symptom. In his essay "After the Catastrophe," a review of the Third Reich, Jung notes that in times of disorder, Germany chose the most disordered among them to be their leader. And he led them, like a pied piper, across the roofs until they fell into the streets below and broke their backs. This is but one historic paradigm whose unlearned lesson is alive and haunting this troubled hour in this troubled nation. Change is never easy. But history tells us that the future belongs to those who can weather change, not resist it. The thing one fears has already happened, and one must now open to it and find the best way to move with it.

There are several takeaways from this moment in history from which each of us may learn. None is reassuring.

1. The "common" values of inclusion and integration of others have proved very fragile, especially as old orders are threatened by change, more foreigners are on "their" turf, and the nervous twitch of interwoven economies prevails.

2. We are, at heart, nonrational beings. We serve whatever complex has been activated in the present hour. The cultural institutions, rationally created to provide both stability and continuity through changing times, are gamed, and the social system continues to privilege the few at the expense of the many. Reason is easily overthrown, the tumbrils are loaded with political corpses, and only the undertaker profits. As Dostoevsky's underground man illustrates, humans love nothing more than to rationalize their irrational beliefs and actions, and anxiety management systems prevail. As psychologists know, we use reason to legitimize our emotional responses and, thanks to the bias toward "confirmation," alter reality to fit our emotional needs.

3. Learning, science, and knowledge are denigrated in favor of a contrived "reality TV." Critical thinking skills are distant memories, if they ever existed. Unquestioned self-interest leads to entrapment within a circle of ignorance, mendacity, and prevarication. When "facts" are unpleasant, one can create "alternative facts." Such a tawdry device may offer a moment's comfort, but it is, ultimately, a psychotic way to make one's critical decisions.

4. As I have noted, we bet on "fear" rather than the issues that legitimately face any culture. Just as investigative journalists used to say, "Follow the money trail," so we can say, "Follow the fear trail" and quickly discern, despite their protestations of piety, what engines of dark design are at work in the lives of most people most of the time.

5. The utility of Jung's concept of the Shadow is more applicable than ever. The Shadow, as we have discussed earlier, includes those parts of ourselves, or our affiliations, which, when brought to consciousness, are found troubling, contradictory to our professions, and yet compelling in our allegiance to them. Most of the time, the Shadow is unconscious, or it is projected onto the Other who must then carry our disowned parts. The Other is so fearsome to us because it reminds us of those parts of ourselves we prefer not to acknowledge. Apparently, one has to create an enemy in the Other because one can so little face the Other within one's own heart.

It is certainly true that anyone—if they felt their core values violated, the prospect of their security and predictability eroded, their cultural history and affiliations bypassed, and the future of their family and children marginalized, even persecuted— would naturally panic and try to reconstitute the old order, the world they once knew and in which they felt secure. And as one's desperation grows, the remedies grow in magnitude.

Why is it so difficult to heal these splits? First, nature equips us with what the military calls IFF systems: "identification friend or foe." Military pilots often have to make life-and-death decisions in tenths of a second about whether the incoming jet is a NATO friendly, a hostile MIG, or their equivalents. Sometimes this decision is now being made "over the horizon," that is, before visual contact is even made. This mechanism in our psyche is critical to survival because that moving branch may prove either a tribal comrade or a waiting tiger. Thus, softening the distinctions between friend and foe often requires overriding instinctual protective mechanisms, which is obviously not easy.

Secondly, the ego is a tiny, fluid island in a shifting sea of energies and is easily overwhelmed. As we know, it tends to privilege its position in order to quell its anxieties, often leading to an unrealistic yet protective inflation. Some of that defensiveness is in all of us, so the Other gets an extra dollop of threat potential at all times.

And lastly, the relationship of the ego to the unconscious is always ambivalent. As Jung put it, "The dread and resistance to entering the unconscious is understandable for it is the voyage to Hades."[5] So much of this either/or polarity is built into our survival mechanisms, and only cross-acculturation, ego maturation, education, travel, and the like can begin to both toughen it and make it more flexible. It is clear that the level of one's, and a culture's, maturity is in due proportion to its capacity to tolerate Otherness. Any Otherness may be experienced with ambiguity and ambivalence, thus triggering anxiety and our protective systems.

The Jungian idea of the Shadow is both personal and collective. Beneath the veneer of the most civilized society lurks the primal powers of the archaic Shadow. As Jung pointed out about Germany in the 1930s, the secret god of the nation was not the Christian God but Wotan.[6] One cannot help but remember that the Nationalsozialistische Deutsche Arbeiterpartei (NASDAP), the Nazi Party, began with six members, one of whom was Hitler. As he was the best speaker of the group, he became the leader, though he was not its founder. He was a miserable tactician as a general but unfortunately brilliant in tapping into the fears of his time.

As Jung noted in 1936,

> There is no lunacy people under the domination of an archetype will not fall prey to. If thirty years ago anyone had dared to predict that our psychological development was tending towards a revival of the medieval persecutions of the Jews, that Europe would again tremble before the Roman fasces and the tramp of legions, that people would once again give the Roman salute, as two thousand years ago, and that instead of the Christian cross an archaic swastika would lure onward millions of warriors ready for death—why that man would have been hooted at as a mystical fool. And today? Surprising as it may seem, all this absurdity is a horrible reality.[7]

Thus, a thousand little grievances grow into a large grudge, which grows into an underground swell, and therein a movement sweeps the stage of history, for a while, until its compensation, its self-proclaimed savior, arrives. As a result, in reaction to the emergence of "feminine" values in recent years, we have a macho leadership cadre; to working-class angst, we have a cabinet of billionaires; to the caring for the earth, we have "Drill, baby, drill"; and to the nuanced respect for human sentiments, we have crude sloganeering, deliberate provocations, and in-your-face politics. So history rolls through reaction and counter-reaction.

It is a difficult but necessary consideration for every one of us in a democracy to consider the health of our leaders. The famous "Goldwater Rule" rose after too many armchair therapists and psychiatrists opined on the candidate's health and mental status back in 1964. Yet today, we see so much more of the candidates and have so much access to information about them and the lives they have led. Privacy is destroyed, and all is out in the open. One cannot help but see what one sees, what has been in one's face since 2016.

Consider the characteristics associated with narcissistic personality disorder, the most common diagnosis offered by psychologists of our former president:

- Grandiosity with expectations of superior treatment from others

- Fixated on phantasies of power, success, intelligence, attractiveness, etc.

- Self-perception of being unique, superior, and associated with high-status people and institutions

- Needing constant admiration from others
- Sense of "entitlement" to special treatment and obedience from others
- Exploitative of others to achieve personal gain
- Unwilling to empathize with others' feelings, wishes, or needs
- Intensely envious of others and believing that others are equally envious of them
- Pompous and arrogant demeanor

Does any of that sound familiar? While aspects of this profile may fit many of our previous presidents, we have to look at our recent and would-be occupant of 1600 Pennsylvania Avenue, Donald Trump, as a poster child for this pathology. It is always a civic duty to examine and monitor our leaders—all of them.

One characteristic of the personality disorder is an inability to look within, to own their Shadow. Rather, they project it onto others, are able to "spin" facts instantaneously to fit their interests, and are incredibly sensitive to any real or perceived slights, to which they usually respond with aggression.[8] Others have argued that the recent president is not a psychological problem but a political problem: an ambitious man with a populist agenda and the skills to maneuver his way through the system. The "solution" to him is not therapy, for he will never be in the consulting room, but political blowback and legal consequences rising from his actions.

So, to answer the questions, is he mentally ill? Is he fit for the most responsible position in the world, the unavoidable answers are yes, he is, and no. The Mayo Clinic, among many others, says narcissistic personality disorder is a mental disorder in which people have an inflated sense of their own importance, a deep need for admiration, and a lack of empathy for others. But behind this mask of ultra-confidence lies a fragile self-esteem that's vulnerable to the slightest criticism. His "false self" is already imperiled in the face of critical scrutiny. Where once he ran his businesses like a medieval lord, brooking no naysayers, now he has to face the press, the intelligence community, the Department of Justice, various subpoenas and indictments, and many inconvenient facts.

So what can one do about all these divisions, this national rancor? Seven thoughts come to me:

1. WORK ON YOURSELF. Here is an example of a man whom I know who lives in Houston, and here is the program of self-examination he has set for himself. I consider his honesty and strength of character, such that he can be honest in looking at himself, to be exemplary for the rest of us. The healing of our split souls, and our split nation, begins with humility. Here is how he addresses himself: "This country is deeply polarized. The divisiveness is frightening to people on both sides. We are all struggling to find out what we can do to heal the wounds. For the last decade I have struggled with the fact that politics and political discussions bring out the worst in me. I don't want to be the way that I am, but I see the following in myself:

- I have become aware of how attached I am to my beliefs and values.

- I find it difficult to listen to opposing views with an open mind.

- This confidence in my personal opinions leads me to a sense of arrogance and self-righteousness.

- The arrogance and self-righteousness lead me to contempt and anger at those who disagree.

- The anger and contempt can destroy my sense of well-being and equanimity."

My hope is that more of us might undertake this work with our personal Shadow. As Jung noted of our necessary Shadow work, everything that is wrong in the world is also wrong in us, and if we begin to address that, we have begun the Tikkun Olam—the healing of our world.

2. SHOW UP AND SPEAK OUT at home and at work when your values are violated. Protest when and where appropriate. Learned helplessness leads to passivity, and passivity leads to lethargy, cynicism, and despair.

3. VOTE.

4. KEEP DOING WHAT YOU DO because the health of the polis depends on you as parents, as caregivers, as citizens. If you are a poet, write; a musician, compose; a mother, mother; a carpenter, pound those nails deep and true; and so on. The work of civilization must be sustained, even as institutions falter and fail. We are all its carriers. We need to

let go of the futile idea that we can control events or people or the vast sweep of history, but we can choose our values, what we stand for, and what we will be attempting to achieve in our short time here.

5. BE KIND because we are all in this together, now and in the times to come. Remember the words of those who lived in troubled times before us. Philo of Alexandria reminded us two millennia ago to be kind, for everyone we meet has a really big problem. Remember that we are dealing with folks for whom their fears are rampant, and we can never find a common ground without empathy toward those fears, real or fanciful as they may be. And, of course, remember, and try to live, the compelling request of the Great Emancipator that we address our neighbor "with malice toward none; with charity for all."

6. BE A SKEPTIC. It is not pessimistic to be distrustful of proclamations of general truths, no matter from whom they emanate; it is realistic. Mencken wrote this in 1930: "Men otherwise highly enlightened cling maudlinly to ideas that go back to the infancy of the human race. Worse, they assume that what they thereby permit themselves to believe, irrationally and against all the known facts, is a kind of knowledge."[9] Skepticism, like doubt, is how we honor serious matters by truly questioning them.

The soul of America may be bankrupt, as its critics allege, but it is not empty. It is full of banalities, junk food, junk ideas, junk science, and a thousand distractions. Anyone who can describe the horrors of slavery as offering folks a useful trade skill from which they might profit, as several state officials did, is either looney or pathologically cynical. Those who, out of ignorance or, more likely, defense of privilege and economic advantage, denied climate science or a rigorous medical approach to COVID-19 have blood on their hands. Many Americans, and others, died as a result of their foot-dragging. Is it not of interest to all of us that the same climate deniers, for example, will arrive at the ER and immediately forswear pseudoscience and ask instead for anaesthesia and the latest medical techniques? When it is one's own body, things get very real, very fast.

7. STAY CONSCIOUS THROUGH IT ALL, with your center as your balancing agency, your place of security. As Emily Dickinson wrote during the Civil War, "The Sailor cannot see the North—but knows the Needle can."[10] She was acutely, and prophetically, aware of the erosion of external and institutional authority and sought to remind each of us that we have an internal guidance system, a de facto compass, that can orient us and lead us to the right choices for us, even if it feels very lonely for a while. Jung takes Dickinson's injunction a step further and suggests that the sole purpose of existence is to kindle the candle of consciousness in the darkness of mere being.

My hope, and my invocation to the reader, is: Keep your candle of consciousness lit, address your own Shadow first before disclaiming the Shadow of others, and keep the fire for freedom, dignity, and respect for all burning with a hot blue flame in your heart.

The lion shall lie down with
the calf, but the calf won't
get very much sleep.

—Woody Allen

7

When You Stare into the Abyss

It is easy to misread Nietzsche. Everyone does it sooner or later. In the 1920s, Leopold and Loeb did. These two brilliant graduate students of philosophy at the University of Chicago began sniffing and snuffing Nietzsche's intoxicating prose and decided that if the superior being, the Übermensch, or "Superior Man," was above the law, then they could demonstrate their exalted status by murdering a child. Bobby Franks, a fourteen-year-old, died in 1924 as a result of their infatuation with the abyss. Only the inspired, passionate defense by Clarence Darrow spared them the electric chair in Joliet. Loeb was subsequently hoisted on a shiv in prison in 1936, but Leopold was released to work with a religious group in 1956 and lived an exemplary life, even providing health care service in his final years. At the time, one of them said he wanted to learn how it felt to be a murderer. He reported that he felt no different from the person he was before. Bobby Frank's death proved not even purposeful; it was, literally, senseless murder and rampant narcissism.

In the recent TV series *The Sinner*, two young men tested themselves as superior beings by also flouting conventional morality, including a murder here and there. In the end, the central character, shot in the stomach by a police officer, died a miserable death. When queried about this sanguinary end, the policemen reported that the young man was consumed by fear during his demise. So much for Nietzsche's bravado-balm along the way.

In the last month, I have lost three dear friends and colleagues going back to childhood and high school, including my dear lifelong comrade Kent. A short while back, given my shaky medical prognosis and eighty-plus years of not-always-easy roads, my wife and I entered a retirement community. It is not really a nursing home, per se, but a place where one owns one's quarters, where one may come and go as one pleases and may attend classes, go on trips, and so on. Still, there is a skilled nursing unit and a memory center. It is not accurate to say that everyone here is waiting to die, for they are a lively and engaged group of folks who have often had distinguished careers and interesting travels. But I cannot ignore the presence of walkers and canes and the fact that questions are raised if a person is not seen at dinner for a day or so. I said to my wife that it was going to require us to get used to living with old folks; she reminded me that we were old folks, so we'd better get used to it. So, as the old vaudevillian intro has it, "I am not only happy to be here with you tonight, I am happy to be anywhere tonight."

In his 1973 classic, *The Denial of Death*, Ernest Becker explores how so much of human behavior is a reaction to the paradox that this animal becomes conscious of its mortality and inevitability and that death is the ultimate sovereign in its capacity to arrive at any time. But this animal also has the capacity to set against its mortal limits a symbolic life that offers some modicum of relief or even transcendence of death. Indeed, Becker argues, most cultures are elaborate, albeit unconscious, means by which the individual or the tribe can escape the finality of death through an afterlife. Of course, if there is an afterlife, it is another life and not this one, hedged as it is with suffering and loss. As Hamlet notes, having shuffled off that mortal coil, no credible traveler has yet returned from that presumptive land to tell us what it is about.

> Learning to live with ambiguity is one sign of the mature personality. Any "certainty" we attain today will, sooner or later, be supplanted by something contradictory or more compelling, and we have to go back to the drawing board.

The erosion of tribal forms of belief and the symbolic systems that once linked folks to some transcendent realm where the gods abide has increased the level of existential anxiety. Accordingly, modern and postmodern Western cultures have evolved a plethora of "treatment plans" as anodynes. Drugs and alcohol have always been with us, but we now possess a wired, 24/7 popular culture available as a distraction. As long ago as the seventeenth century, mathematician and mystic Blaise Pascal noted that the court had invented the jester as a distraction so that it would not ponder its existential dilemma and grow morose. He called this phenomenon *divertissement*, or "diversion." How much more available and sophisticated the distractions have grown, precisely in proportion to the decline of traditional religion. Our frenetic culture, rushing somewhere and hoping to get there quickly, is essentially fleeing death anxiety. One might follow the wisdom of sagacious Satchel Paige, who said, "Don't look back. Something might be gaining on you,"[1] but, as Shakespeare's Richard II reminds us in Act III, one doesn't get very far in one's flight:

> For within the hollow crown
> That rounds the mortal temples of a king
> Keeps Death his court, and there the antic sits,
> Scoffing his state and grinning at his pomp,
> Allowing him a breath, a little scene,
> To monarchize, be feared, and kill with looks,
> Infusing him with self and vain conceit,
> As if this flesh which walls about our life,
> Were brass impregnable; and humour'd thus
> Comes at the last and with a little pin
> Bores through his castle wall, and farewell, king!

Becker's cultural analysis deconstructs the popular views of "the good life," with all its distractions, blandishments, and shiny seductions, in such pseudo-religions as hedonism, consumerism, and addiction. The progressive retreat of former symbolic systems in the face of scientific method and discoveries; travel and education, which enlarge one's experience beyond the tribe; the deconstructions of social structures, once thought either ontological or divinely ordained; and empiricisms of all kinds have abetted the shifting of the ground beneath our feet. As a result, popular fads, fashions, and pursuits of trivialities fill the gap, or try to. All of these apparent choices from the palette of activities serve as "terror management" systems, as some have described the effort to negotiate a rapprochement between the ego's desire for perpetuation and the inevitability and unpredictability of its demise.

Similarly, Irvin D. Yalom's *Staring at the Sun* explores what happens, and what one's options are, when one awakens, fully awakens, to one's tenuous hold on this life. He supports the life-affirming goals that may rise from this otherwise debilitating terror. We are called to decide what our priorities really are, treasure our relationships with those whom we love, and step more fully into the risks necessary to pursue that for which our soul longs.

Recent medical challenges in my life, including radiation, chemotherapy, and some risky surgeries, have brought this issue to the forefront. I found myself accepting my death, for what other honest choice is there, really? But I also found myself swimming in large emotions regarding not leaving my companion bride and our adult children alone. Further, I still value my work, and I am still a person of insatiable curiosity, ranging from learning more and more about art to the richness of current discoveries in archaeology, anthropology, astronomy, and the sundry disciplines of the humanities, which never fail to enlarge, inform, and open me to the next set of questions. In other words, there is still much for which to live.

Learning to live with ambiguity is one sign of the mature personality. Any "certainty" we attain today will, sooner or later, be supplanted by something contradictory or more compelling, and we have to go back to the drawing board. This is how we grow, how we stay in relationship to the essential mysteries of life. I am drawn, even as I am daunted, by Rilke's reminder that we need to be continuously defeated by ever-larger things. What I surmise Rilke is driving toward is that if we are taking on newer and newer challenges, we will frequently be "defeated" from an ego standpoint, but we are living a larger life in so doing.

More and more I believe that the concept identified by Hans Vaihinger in 1911 in his book *Die Philosophie des Als Ob* (*The Philosophy of the "As If"*) offers a narrow isthmus between these yawning polarities. One may consciously adopt a point of view, attitude, practice *as if* it were universally true, for this move helps one focus one's energies and, most importantly, gives one a purposeful relationship to our limited condition and provides purpose to how we spend our energy.

This concept of the "useful fiction" serves as a catalyst to both practical and attitudinal changes and commitments. Socrates once noted that he did not know if there was such a thing as immortality, but the subject was so compelling to him that it gave him a life's work. Similarly, a caregiver may understand that she or he may not save the other, or even her- or himself, but that tenderness, compassion, and insight toward others who suffer are values that seem inherently rewarding. Of course one can, as seen previously, adopt the fictive assignment of filling one's house with gold, only to find that loving the metallic proves sterile.

So we are obliged to choose our "fictions" carefully. I am only partly invested these days in whether Jungian or analytic psychology will survive, but I do know that for the last half-century it has provided me with a lens and a frame through which I have had a meaningful few decades and whose efficacy persists to this hour. Woody Allen once observed that he wanted to achieve immortality not through his work but through not dying. Someone said to me a few years ago that my works would continue through my books, and I replied that I expect that they will grow unread one generation after my departure. In other words, I do not expect immortality through any effort of my own, nor do I want that at this stage. After all, I am dead, hors de combat. What might matter to me now will not matter at all then.

The pragmatic question confronting us each day, whether we attend consciously or not, is "What does my mortal condition make me do or keep me from doing?" I assert that that question spurs one out of the doldrums to action and commitment to something. The key is that one knows that it does not alter one's fundamental mortal condition, but that what remains of life is more fully lived.

When we reflect that the mortal cycle drives all of nature, including us, we then may question why it is we think we merit exemption from the turn of the iron wheel. Death is not a problem for nature or, apparently, Divinity, but it is a problem for ego consciousness that seeks its own perpetuation. How often do we ask ourselves, "Why should I live longer—sucking oxygen and polluting the environment as I unavoidably do—other than to gratify the ego? Should I live longer than someone else, and why?" While we need that ego for the conduct of daily life, the ego, sensing its vulnerability, assumes the inflationary attitude that it is in charge and has special privilege. The development of modern medicine and surgery, for which I am extremely grateful, has significantly furthered the notion that life can, and should, be extended indefinitely, so will I be capable of saying, when the proverbial guy with the scythe and hourglass shows at my door, "It is my turn now. I am not exempt. I surrender to the great turning of the wheel"? I hope I can.

For more and more Western moderns, given the brutal fact of death, the promises of an afterlife appear less and less convincing. Hence, an increasing number have turned to the practices of Buddhism, which emphasize that the ego's attitude and compulsive attachment are the chief causes of our suffering. Relinquishing the phantasy of mastery over life is the task, but how many of us achieve that level of insight and perhaps courage? How many of us reflexively slip into fortifications of the ego's stockade, armed against the encroachment of the great cycle of things?

I suspect we best deal with the great abyss, the Abgrund, or "ground-falling-away," as the German word expresses it, by living with this paradox of immortal longing hedged by mortal limits, and not by engaging in distractions or metaphysical sleights of hand to finesse the dilemma. Martin Heidegger once defined the abyss as "the openness of Being." That reframes matters nicely. The abyss is not just that which confronts and intimidates; it is that which opens to infinite possibility. This opening to the larger has produced both Beethoven's Ninth Symphony and the tawdry, soulless zones of pinball palaces with flashes of light, noise, and blessed distraction.

Any understanding we have of this mystery today, any coping strategy, will be undone tomorrow when we awake with a mysterious ache in the side or a CAT scan with threatening shadows. So we have to accept that this life is a rolling crapshoot, with the odds decidedly against "winning." In the end, the meaning of our lives is not found in surviving. We don't. But it does matter how we lived this life in the meantime. The psyche of those in the final process dreams not of endings but of crossings, journeys. One wonders what the depths of our souls may know that we don't. It little matters what we think, but it does matter how we live this short pause between two great mysteries. Aligning ourselves with that open-ended mystery may be what the ancients called wisdom and what therapeutic traditions call healing.

In the meantime, there are many ways of dying, and death is only one of them. Typically, there are many deaths daily. We all may die when fear governs our lives or when we don't really show up for life's difficulties. We die when we choose security over exploration and discovery. We especially die when we choose palliative "certainties" over inconvenient and troubling quiddities.

Remember Nietzsche's warning that those who stare into the abyss should know that the abyss also stares into them. Still, not to have approached the edge and looked therein is not to have been here at all, or to have been here in the most superficial way. We recover the depth and dignity of the journey upon which the soul is embarked when we remember that the point is to have been here, to have opened to the wonder and terror of it all, and to have expressed our soul's intent as best we could.

We must laugh and we must sing,
We are blest by everything,
Everything we look upon is blest.

—W. B. Yeats

8

Die Traumdeutung der Trauma

The Meaning of Trauma

Life is inherently traumatic. Sleeping through the aeons, all needs met, the infant is violently expelled from an Edenic state, is flung into the contingent world of nature naturing, and ends in its demise. The meaning and effects of traumatic experience will vary from person to person, from context to context, and from mitigating environment to uncertain setting. While this human animal is gifted with an amazing power to adjust, develop, and carry on the task of life, the imprint of trauma lingers in all of us.

Perhaps the simplest definition of trauma is "the experience of more units, more quanta of experience than ego consciousness can assimilate at that time." Trauma is also defined as having experiences larger than our Weltanschauung, or "worldview," can frame, define, or treat at that time. A good example of the latter is the suffering of Job. While his various losses were traumatic enough, the largest trauma was that his whole way of understanding self and cosmos was eclipsed, demolished even, by the catastrophic encounter with the wild God that demolished his inherited theology. No longer could he believe what he once believed, beliefs that comforted him and provided him with a sense of agency in the world. From that moment onward, Job had to experience his spiritual nakedness before the powers of an unknowable and unmanageable universe. Similarly, the doctrine of meliorism, which animated the beliefs of many at the turn of the twentieth century, disappeared in the butchery of the trenches at Passchendaele in The Great War. The philosophy of moral and social improvement, if enough folks put their shoulders to that wheel, was shattered by the slaughters of the Somme River, in which, for example, the British suffered sixty thousand casualties in one twenty-four-hour period. Modern civilization, as Ezra Pound described, was "an old bitch gone rotten in the teeth."[1] The doctrine of social "progress" would never be the same thereafter.

Many experiences of life are traumatic. The early psychoanalysts made much of birth trauma. Each infant encounters the twin threats of overwhelmment and abandonment that dog us our entire lives. Much in life looms larger than our capacity to manage it all, and all of us from time to time feel, as in the words of the old spiritual, "like a motherless child," alone and adrift amid the eddies and anarchic currents of outer and inner experience. All of us, from time to time, are flushed with feelings of helplessness, powerlessness, humiliation, even depersonalization. Perhaps no one depicted these existential states as dramatically as Prague's Franz Kafka in stories such as "The Hunger Artist" and "The Penal Colony" and in the novella *The Metamorphosis*, among others.

As we have noted earlier, the psyche seems to have two agendas at all times: healing and enlarged expression of the soul's intent. Something within each of us seeks repair, restoration, and reframing via sleep and dreams and the development of a core resilience. Sabina Spielrein, for example, asserted that our creative, imaginative capacity is one of the primary modes whereby humankind develops alternative approaches to the traumatizing elements by reframing and redeeming images. Just think of the subject matter of so much popular music that laments the loss of the Beloved, the flight from familiar places and people, and the hope of renewal. Sleep research tells us that up to one-third of our life is spent in restorative sleep and six years dreaming out of eighty years alive, "knit[ting] up the raveled sleave of care," as Shakespeare put it.[2] Even through somatic seizures and flashbacks, the psyche seeks to process and dispel the traumatic content and recover the Edenic ecology of the undamaged soul.

Traumatic events are incorporated into the body, as Bessel van der Kolk traces in *The Body Keeps the Score*. One's neurology activates the fight/flight/freeze range of behaviors, which, over time, become characteristic patterns of reflexive response not only to the original traumata but to other venues in which an analogue is triggered. If one felt, for example, smothered by a pathogenic parent, often the defensive perimeter created will extend to other relationships as a preemptive protection.

The phenomenological event, the trauma itself, which may be wordless or imageless, generally triggers an epiphenomenal image and a fragmentary narrative. The sensitive psyche asks of the experience, "What was that?" and "What does it mean?" and "How am I to understand that?" and, perhaps most compelling, "What does that make me do or keep me from doing?" This last, epiphenomenal question is a critical heuristic inquiry that can help free one from bondage to the traumata and their recurrent affective ripples and recover a measure of freedom. One of the sequelae of trauma is typically a hypervigilance to sounds, sights, and triggering associations. While protective in its intent, hypervigilance means that one is "wired" to one's sensorium and overly reactive in one's responses to the world of sights and sounds around one.

As we know, part of the treatment for trauma may employ tranquilizing medications, the reenactment of the traumata in a safe environment, and desensitization rituals. The role of psychotherapy is to identify and isolate the "stories" that rise from our experiences and bind us to the trauma. Our "stories" rise from our human need to make sense of our lives and animate events in service to some possible understanding.

Each of us assembles a de facto false self— "false" because it's reactive to life's traumata and not generated from the Self as such. One of the ways we begin to discern and trace the outlines of our traumata is from the adaptive patterns we evolve from early childhood onward. We all have variant "treatment" patterns, including dissociation, compliance, codependence, and aggression. These patterns are the lineaments of trauma's presence and our responses to them. What rises from these adaptive behaviors is a protective system that, ironically, can separate us further from ourselves. The very adaptations that protect us have a tendency to take on larger and larger roles in our self-governance. In fact, one might observe that the greater the traumatic experience, the greater the protective response— fight, flight, freeze, accommodate, and so on—becomes. Paradoxically, that which offers a modicum of protection is also a wedge between our natural, instinctually driven selves and our employment of stratagems that separate us from our souls. In its simplest form, the more we have to adapt to whatever is happening "out there," the less we are connecting to what is spontaneous and generative "in here."

Central to the work of psychoanalysis is the identification of one's "stories" and how they become reflexive life-management scripts. Avoid, engage, placate, whatever the message—the assemblage of protective mechanisms takes on a life of its own.

Accordingly, one's adaptive measures are often the constricting powers of history that infiltrate and channel the responses of today. All of us tend to identify who we are with what happened to us. So, for example, if we have experienced derogating voices in our development, we either subscribe to them ourselves or spend our lives compensating for them. These lifelong adaptive protections constitute the warp and woof of our self-story, but they are derived from how we responded to something rather than who we are. Cultural traumata, such as racism, sexism, ageism, and so on, potentially define a person for a lifetime if left unconscious and unchallenged.

Each of us is summoned to declare over and over, "I am not what happened to me. I am what I choose to become." Or alternatively, "I am what wants to enter the world through the fuller expression of my soul." Unless that declaration is repeated many times, the old, reflexive protections will reassert their debilitating enactments.

But how do we ever know we are not what happened to us? That our stories are not our realities? Well, for one thing, we sometimes, often perhaps, simply outgrow them. The demands of maturing, as well as the inherent resiliency of the psyche, often move beyond these old protections. We learn other, perhaps more efficacious modes of coping with life's distresses. We have compensatory dreams that call attention to the stuck places, the old haunts and hauntings. We have psychopathology that rises spontaneously to protest even our protections and endorse whatever wishes us to operate from a different premise than the stories formulated so long ago. And sometimes we simply have to muster courage to face life's demands and bend our convictions and will toward something larger than our history. In those hours we find something within that supports us.

In a homey metaphor, Jung noted that we all walk in shoes too small for us. That is to say, we all walk in the mincing steps of powerlessness, fear, and need for consensus. One former client, referred by a judge for her DUI, said she did not understand what the idea of a "higher power" was until she realized in an AA meeting that her higher power to that point was a bottle. That, she knew, was something too small for the conduct of her life. At that moment, she began to grow up and take over the adult's responsibility for her life.

Complexes are those clusters of energy that lie coiled within each of us, waiting to be triggered to then enact their narrative instructions. We all have complexes because we all have a life history, and life charges each of us with signal encounters that must be engaged. Regrettably, complexes have no imagination. They can only repeat their old, dreary, reductive message: run, hide, make nice, whatever. But our dreams, our psychopathology, and our impulses to evolve all come from a larger, more imaginative energy that flows from the Self, the superordinate center of the personality. The conflict between these two force fields within us, the need for protection and the need for growth and expression, occurs within each of us throughout the arc of our lives.

These adaptive "protections" reduce the range of our expressive capacities. Thus, inadvertently, we become our own worst enemies. As Jung noted, our greatest Shadow issue is not that we are evil but that we tend to live lives too small for the soul's more capacious horizon. Remember, the three tasks the "witch" figure sent the dreamer in the earlier chapter—make love with a fat man, go to the university to deliver a lecture, and have a charged dinner with the witch's deputy stepmother—were all in service to the larger life envisioned by the Self and not the traumata of the dreamer's childhood experience. Freud tended, in my opinion, to be too optimistic that an identification of the origin of a trauma and its attendant behaviors would often suffice to liberate the blocked libido, and life could move forward. In fact, the power of the complex is such that we can become its lifelong slaves. Jung was nearer the truth when he said we don't solve these stuck places, but we can outgrow them.

Like Ixion bound to his fiery wheel, our complexes dictate the repetition compulsion, and the pattern is reinforced. It is even possible, we think, to transcend the complex and its limiting powers precisely through experiencing them over and over, but more likely, each repetition binds us to that wheel of necessity even more firmly. In conversation many years ago with a former director of a Holocaust museum, I learned of the high incidence of mortality among the survivors of the concentration camps in the years immediately after liberation. One can certainly posit a compromised immune system as one factor that leads in that direction, but my colleague and I also concluded that what those folks had witnessed was a form of soul-murder, from which one does not recover easily. As Job experienced, when one's lived experience shatters the frame of one's understanding of self and world, one's hold on life itself grows tenuous and imperiled. We have to believe in something, and if that something is only darkness, then our soul's sovereignty is at risk.

Paradoxically, it is also possible that our wounds, our traumata, may quicken consciousness and cause us to become especially sensitive to, and acutely focused upon, the iatrogenic character of our experience. So the wounded healer is often especially gifted in empathizing with the suffering of others, although opening one's wound to the wound of others is risky business and can lead to inordinate stress and self-anaesthetizing treatment plans. In such moments, one also has to ask a potentially liberating question: Does my own trauma bind me to this work with others like Ixion to his wheel of repetition, or is this really my calling that rises out of the detritus of traumatic experience? Not to know the difference between these two sources can be the difference between vocation and onerous labor, between freedom of choice and iron determinism.

As Jung noted, behind the wound often lies the genius of the person as she or he becomes especially sensitive, especially adapted to the work, but from the outside, one cannot tell which power is greater—calling or compulsion. Ultimately, for any of us to get our lives back, to move from reactivity to generativity, we have to face our fears. What was overwhelming to the child is still problematic to the adult, although the latter has powers, choices, options, and resiliency that the child lacked. The counter-phobic move is essential as we face our fears as long as we do not take them too literally. Every year, people die because they engage in risky behavior simply because they are afraid and believe that drawing near the fire will be liberating. Sometimes, it rather means one gets burned.

Yet, even when broken by the trauma and its sequelae, one still has to find courage, will, and persistence to show up in life. In other writing, I mentioned that I have a de facto motto I say to myself every day: Shut up; suit up; show up! The first admonition is a reminder that life's ordinary problems do not matter much compared to the genuine suffering of those intractably ill or those deprived of shelter and safety, and so on. So "Shut up" is my reminder not to whine. "Suit up" means to prepare, do one's necessary homework, and not expect an easy path in life. "Show up" means that one simply must do one's best in the face of challenges. None of us escape this life alive, so we do well to do our best to be alive while we are here. While life is always going to be traumatic, it can also be beautiful at times. And we need to be sure that we showed up here as best we could.

The key to the reparation of the psyche is as follows:

- Remember, we are not what happened to us. We are what we wish to become and what wishes to enter life through us.

- We need to bring the epiphenomenal story to consciousness lest its sovereignty over us continue unchallenged.

- We need to see that our stories are fictions, constructs to make sense of experience. Often that sense is reductive and not only denies our resilient powers but binds us to a disabling history.

- We need to ask our stories what they make us do or keep us from doing. This identification is a major step in getting one's life back. Often the story is invisible, but the behavior is visible and what is rendered visible is something consciousness can attend to, challenge, and transcend.

- We need to realize that our reflexive behaviors and stories are epiphenomena and are not the work of the soul itself. Something within each of us is much larger and calls for our accountability. And something within will support us when we step into the larger shoes that life asks of us. In his letter to a young poet, Rilke reminds us that we are set down in life as the element to which we most belong. Life is not something alien. We are its repository, its carrier.

- We need to remember that not everything gets healed, that justice is not always the outcome, and that the work of healing may take a lifetime.

This means we may have to live with matters unresolved, with injustice reverberating in our splintered bones, and the discrepancies between what we wish for our lives and what is achievable are often very great indeed. Accordingly, we all have to live with loss and treasure what we can wrest from it. We have to live with disappointment and savor how blessed we are. We have to live with unachievable desires and be grateful for how they helped us move more fully into life and its struggles.

In *A Portrait of the Artist as a Young Man*, James Joyce wrote that history was a nightmare from which he was trying to awaken. Healing from trauma is awakening from that splintering experience and realizing that there are enough tasks remaining today, in this present life (and more will arrive tomorrow), to consume our energy, and that life goes on asking us to shut up, suit up, show up, and address what each day brings us as best we can. A concise way to put this is "How now, in the face of this which is beyond my control, am I to live my life?" This question moves us from victimhood to active governance of our lives.

Trauma is as unavoidable as breathing, but the human organism has evolved through the millennia and is built to survive and thrive. Rather than be caught in the "story" the trauma dictates, we have to serve the larger story that life is seeking to embody through us. The healing of trauma is best found when we serve that larger story, a story that is so much greater than the splintering that fractious experience crazes within us. We are not what happened to us; we are the sum of how we respond to the summons to be the carrier of new life out of the spectral shadowlands of the past.

In the end, we do not solve life; rather, life slowly unwinds us. The problems of life, the brutality of life, are more than we can master, but we are always left with the summons to do what we can. As a Samuel Beckett character says, "Ever tried. Ever failed. No matter. Try again. Fail again. Fail better."[3]

9

Dark Divinity

The Problem of Evil, the Problem of Good

We begin with an enduring question: Is evil real, is it "psychological," or is it both? I recall a patient in a psychiatric hospital who requested to be put in restraints every morning, that is, tied in sheets to her bed for the day. Most of us would bristle at the loss of our freedom, our mobility, but it was reassuring to her that she would not have to make any choices that day, not engage in her life but be protected from it. When asked why, she told me incredible stories about her mother's torture of her, including putting lit matches under her fingernails. I suspected that such stories were part of her psychotic phantasies, but when I worked through her three-inch-thick file, I found that all her stories, and worse, had been documented as factual. That anyone would have tortured a child as she had been struck me as complete evil, although I never forgot what distorted shape her parent's psyche must have been to relate to her child that way. And in another city in which I lived, another mother, under the influence of fundamentalist shaming and fearmongering, drowned her five children in the bathtub to save them from "the Devil."

Is this capacity for darkness in all of us? Is it caused by a malevolent deity, bad chemistry, really bad parenting, or all of the above? In his collection of essays *Resistance, Rebellion, and Death*, Albert Camus writes:

> We are *faced* with evil. As for me, I feel rather as Augustine did before becoming a Christian where he said, "I tried to find the source of evil and got nowhere." But it is also true that I, and a few others, *know* what must be done, if not to reduce evil, at least not to add to it. Perhaps we cannot prevent this world from being a world in which children are tortured. But we *can* reduce the number of tortured children.

Whatever the nature of nature, or the nature of the archaic gods, one thing that's clear is that "evil" is *our* issue, not theirs. As a character in *The Grapes of Wrath* by John Steinbeck says, "There ain't no sin and there ain't no virtue. There's just stuff people do."[1] The ancient Xenophanes reminded us that if horses and lions could draw, their images of their gods would be horses and lions. As we will see in the last chapter of this book, it is our imago Dei, our images of the gods, that cause us mischief. Most of our images construe a god of justice, compassion, and equity even as our experience of daily life is quite different. We often make a distinction between natural and moral evil, the former being in the nature of nature's nature, showing up as hurricanes or metastatic cancer, and the latter rising from the choices we make from our complex-driven egos and the many promptings that pile up in our separate and collective lives.

In 1755, at the height of Sunday services on All Soul's Day, the ground of Lisbon, Portugal, shook, the structures collapsed, and about sixty thousand souls were crushed under their houses of worship. How was that to be understood? Most thought of the horror as a statement from God about the moral failings of the people who were ostensibly judged. But this is still a stretch when one considers how many children and other unfortunates were beneath those collapsing ceilings.

> The Evil One is gone,
> but the evil ones remain.

The problem of evil is most acute for those who are "theists," that is, those who seek to bundle both good and evil and a moral nature into their image of divinity. It is less a problem for the polytheist. So there is divisiveness, good and evil? No problem. The multiplicities of gods, namely, the personified energies of the universe, simply do their thing, and any contradictions are merely in the confused head of the humans. Dualistic traditions envision a force for good and a force for evil contending through history, with the hope that the former will prevail at the end of time. Most of the American Founding Fathers were "deists," those who, given the created world, imagine a Creator, one who set this marvelous, intricate machine in motion with its wheels and springs but now lets it all run according to its programmings. They emphasized the role of science and education to discern the nature of those contending forces and live in as much harmony with them as possible. For the atheist, or the agnostic, the one who believes there is insufficient evidence to stake a belief position one way or the other, the matter is irresolvable, and our contentions tell us more about ourselves than about the gods.

The classical religions of the East, Hinduism and Buddhism, address evil in a different way. Hinduism asserts that multiple divine forces are contending in nature and in our bodies, and will be so contending throughout history. We are obliged to address the cumulative consequences that we have received and do our best to lift their consequences off of the next incarnation of history. For the Buddhist, evil is an illusion, and the ego is summoned to relinquish its presumptive sovereignty and live as simply and as consciously as possible in harmony with nature but without the expectations of the ego that it can work it all out, or that there is a resolution to the dilemma. The believer is asked to surrender phantasies of management for acceptance and surrender.

For the major religions of the Western world—Judaism, Christianity, and Islam—the inherent contradiction is between their image of Divinity as just, omniscient (knowing all that is really going on), omnipotent (able to change anything as needed), loving, compassionate, and involved, even as life, as it is experienced by most humans most of the time, is a heartbreaking, unresolved perplexity.

As we all have experienced at some moment of peril, we try to make deals with the universe, seeking relief from whatever distress of the hour in return for proffering better comportment from us. Seldom does this search for a quid pro quo work, but that does not keep the reflexive part of our minds from seeking deals the next time. You may recall the story of the grandmother who buys her grandson a baseball cap and takes him to see the ocean for the first time. Of course, the child walks too far out into the surf and is swept seaward. Grandmother is panicked and looks upward and promises God that she will donate all her wealth to charities if only the grandchild might be restored. In a few moments, he is kicked up on the littoral, coughing but alive, whereupon the grandmother looks up at the heavens, shakes her fist, and says, "He had a new cap on too, you know!"

A little under three millennia ago, an unknown Jewish author critiqued the notion of such dealmaking and undermined our presumptive idea of a de facto contract with the cosmos. Job is a pious soul, always minding the law and behaving properly, always expecting God to reciprocate as the First Gentleman He was supposed to be. But such an expectation is overthrown as Job experiences loss of family, wealth, property, and health. In the end, Job recognizes his unwitting hubris and confesses his inflation. In effect, he has moved from a human-driven phantasy about the universe to an actual religious experience of the inexhaustible mystery of the cosmos. In a letter, Jung writes, "God is a mystery, and everything we say about it is said and believed by human beings. We make images and concepts, and when I speak of God, I always mean the images man has made of him. But no one knows what God is like, or he would be a god himself."[2] Put another way, it is humans, not gods, who make theology, and their constructs reveal more about them than about the inexplicable mystery of the great vacant spaces through which they wander.

The history of this question, Jung observes, is the track through the progressive "humanization" of the imago Dei. Slowly the image of a jealous god evolves (of whom would a god have to be jealous, one wonders); a tribal god favoring the home team against the visitors; a vengeful god who, surprisingly, seems to hate the same folks we hate; an amoral god; and an unconscious god. What evolves, then, is not the mystery we call god but our images pointing in that direction.

Accordingly, we see that theology and its multiplicitous variations often tell us more about the humans who generated those images than about the mystery itself. We get so captivated by our own constructs that we are willing to defend them to the death if ever subject to contradictions that inject an unwelcome anxiety into our systems.

Nothing is more to be feared than the person convinced he or she is right, morally superior, and given the instruments of power. Consider this angry poem I wrote many years ago after reading the horrific *Malleus Maleficarum*, or *The Hammer of Witches*, a manual published to help religious authorities identify, interrogate, and extirpate "witches" in their community. The horrors perpetrated by their piety still appalls. The projection of the disowned Shadow on these poor women tells us so little about them and, ironically, so much about their abusers.

What one sees over the recent centuries is the progressive relocation of the origin of moral evil from the unfathomable to the heart and soul of humans. When Goethe's Faust encounters Mephistopheles, he presumes he is meeting Satan, but he is told that whole idea of the Evil One is supplanted now by humankind's capacity for evil. The Evil One is gone, but the evil ones remain, Mephistopheles announces. Evil is democratized and found in the soul of moderns. Dostoevsky portrays the first antihero in his *Notes from Underground*, a person whose confession of narcissism is so unnerving because it's so familiar. And in *Heart of Darkness*, Joseph Conrad reveals the hidden Shadow agenda in the "March of Civilization" that pretends to bring progress to the undeveloped parts of the world but is in fact a land and resource grab camouflaged by rationalizations. Albert Camus explores this self-estrangement in his novel *The Fall*, in which we realize that the closest repository of self-serving evil is within us also. While we profess we would love to go back and

The Hammer of Witches (1486)

Reading the *Malleus Maleficarum* one night
certain observations about witches are vouchsafed:
the subject's private parts may be shaved
lest instruments of dark device be closeted there;
the suspect may be tortured repeatedly
till the body howls for God, any god,
and then be questioned separate from that terrible room,
lest her sudden song seem strained;
the subject may request to clasp a fiery iron
to a count of six—entire gospels
may be memorized in that transit to six.

Most of all, because she is she,
she proves susceptible to noxious designs:
souring children in the womb,
stealing the penis in the carnal act,
deforming cattle, and bringing forth hailstones.

The enormity of her crime is all the greater
for the fragility of her vessel.
She is most culpable, it appears,
for lacking the nobler, sterner stuff
of those who wield the hammer.

make other choices in life, we are secretly grateful we don't have to, for we would make the same choices again in service to the same self-serving complexes. And in Archibald MacLeish's play in verse, *J.B.*, a modern version of Job, his three comforters are a fundamentalist who harangues with the old message of sin and salvation, a Freudian analyst who diagnoses evil as arising from bad parenting, and a Marxist who sees it all as a class struggle for a larger piece of the pie.

Similarly, in her challenging *Eichmann in Jerusalem*, Hannah Arendt coins the phrase "the banality of evil." She went to the trial of the Nazi administrator, half expecting to see a Devil's tail protruding from his coat, and finds instead a bald, bespectacled man whose defense is that he was a humble civil servant whose chief crime was to keep the trains running on time. That those railway cars carried humans to their appointments with the crematoria was the concern of paygrades higher than his. Thus the "banality" was not the magnitude of evil but rather the implementation of a system by ordinary, banal folks like us who keep evil systems going.

We can now see how the Third Reich emerged in Germany, not as a unique one time event but as something even stable societies can suffer when difficult social situations weaken the ego's sense of management and bring about both depression and heightened anxiety. This painful reality can, and often does, lead to the attribution of causal factors to others in order to distance oneself from one's own summons to larger consciousness.

In his article "Degrees of Evil," published in *The Atlantic* in 2002, Ron Rosenbaum links the "motiveless malignancy" of Hitler and cronies laughing at the "rumors" of gas chambers with the hilarity of Osama bin Laden laughing with his accomplices at the amount of gasoline in the tanks of the airliners that brought down the towers in Manhattan. This convergence of enjoyed malignancy, Rosenbaum suggests, produces a symbolic handshake across the decades, not between monsters but between ordinary people doing monstrous things.

If there is a "Jungian" position on evil, it recognizes that when there is too much morality in the outer world, evil goes inward and operates as it will through the unconscious. Jung's concept of the Shadow is that the whole of humanity and its capacity for good and for evil is carried within each of us as our received human lineage. As the Roman playwright Terence said over two millennia ago, nothing human is alien to us. Thus, I should never conclude I am exempt from evil, no matter how well-intentioned my conscious life might be. First because we can never really see down the line to the consequences of our choices, we can never presume ourselves free of complicity. The ubiquity and the moral challenge the Shadow brings to each of us ensure that there will likely be an effort to keep it at bay by remaining unconscious most of the time. Secondly, we will all find in ourselves a willing readiness to see the problem as caused by someone other rather than own it ourselves. Thirdly, because the Shadow is rich life energy, it will, from time to time, rise and possess us, and we will enjoy riding its crest (what happens in Vegas stays in Vegas). Or we may occasionally own that material within us and thereby free up the world in an infinitesimal way from carrying our disowned agendas.

If we are dismayed by our ongoing capacity for evil, we must also be moved by and responsible for our capacity for good. In the end, good and evil are human categories. The gods and/or nature may not be concerned with these categorical opposites at all, but we are.

In his nineteenth-century essay "A Defence of Poetry," Percy Bysshe Shelley concludes that the chief moral agency of the good is the imagination. Those suffering narcissistic and/or sociopathic personality disorders have a diminished capacity for imagination and therefore can only repeat the dreary cycle of the core complexes at the center of their disorder. As we saw before, complexes have no imagination. Fortunately, the bulk of humanity retains the power to imagine and, therewith, feel the suffering of the other. This capacity is what generates compassion (*passio*), empathy, and sympathy (*pathos*)—"passio" and "pathos" being the words for suffering in Latin and Greek respectively. The diminished imagination of the personality disorder, or the pervasive complex, can only pursue its limited self-serving agenda. The enlarged imagination of the thoughtful, sensitive person can reach out and embrace the world and its suffering, as the word *Weltschmerz* suggests.

To know evil is the task of the human brain. To cope with it is the summons of the human heart. And most of us are strung out along humanity's long procession pursuing this alternating thread through history. Apparently, good and evil are not categories of divinity or nature, but they are the daily arena in which we find the gyroscope of the soul seeking to find its balance and hold to principles that either lead into or out of the valley of the Shadow.

I've always been worried about my damn soul—maybe I worry too much. But you carry in one hand a bundle of darkness that accumulates each day. And when death finally comes, you say right away, "Hey, buddy, glad to see ya!"

—Charles Bukowski

10

Bundles of Darkness/ Moments of Meeting

The Despoiled and Present State of the Soul

A ll we have to do is look around to see the sad state of affairs: a broken treaty with nature, partisanship and animosity, and self-estrangement that leads to distance from others. When we survey the post–World War II religious landscape of the United States, only two forms of deliberate religious observance have grown, while all of the mainstream institutions have declined in size and influence. One evokes the negative parent complex in their flocks, making them frightened, docile, manageable, and mindless. The other stream, which has flourished, promises that if and when one gets right with the Big Guy upstairs, one will be blessed with health, wealth, and happiness. The former intimidates, the latter seduces. Both are thoughtless efforts to manipulate fear and uncertainty, manage the mystery, and fill their coffers. Both will fail their congregants in the long run.

One finds much more religious honesty in the raggedy poems of Charles Bukowski, who tried to write his way back to his own soul. In his poem "A Smile to Remember," he writes that his mother told him that "it's better to be happy if you can /

but my father continued to beat her and me several times a week while / raging inside his six-foot-two frame because he couldn't / understand what was attacking him from within."

Was there ever a psychologist, or Jungian analyst, with a better etiological diagnosis than that? One thing abided amid the sundry distresses of Bukowski's life: writing. He intuitively knew that writing was his dearest, best approach to all that pain and self-mortification that dictated his outer life. No aesthetic transcendence for him, no Rilkean or Yeatsean sleights of hand. He dove into the mess and emerged with new wounds and a peculiar sense of glory for having spoken his truth, however tawdry and demeaning it might seem. Writing in Patterson, New Jersey, William Carlos Williams once concluded that a man stalking the gutter has more dignity than the priest in his high church gowns. Rather than emerge from services evincing a smug ownership of the mystery, a surreptitious deal struck with the powers of the universe, such poets as Bukowski have more spiritual integrity and depth than the most satisfied congregant. As T. S. Eliot wrote of another poète maudit, Charles Baudelaire "earned" damnation, a spiritual testing that came to the honestly wretched, marking them with a badge of authenticity denied to the comfortable. As Eliot put it, our "glory" is just as much found in our capacity for damnation as in our capacity for salvation. As one thoughtful cleric once said, "My job is to bring comfort to the afflicted and affliction to the comfortable."

Writing over a century ago, in *Symbols of Transformation*, Jung differentiated two kinds of thinking: linear and associational.[1] The former leads to logic, sequence, conclusion. The latter leads wherever it wants to go, including madness. I once waited for a tram on a rainy street in Zürich while I was in training there. From a nearby school, a procession of children, all clad in yellow slickers, came traipsing down Hölderlinstrasse.

Their appearance, like a famous Ezra Pound poem, was of yellow petals on a wet black bough. Their sweet song, on a street named for a poet who went mad, was both discordant and congruent, and I thought even at the time it was somehow worth remembering. Life, or bad chemistry, broke Hölderlin, but these children were singing before life would have its way with them. I recall that image as a bridge between the madness and the beauty of that moment. So, too, while I sat in the boathouse adjacent to the C. G. Jung-Institut in a personal dark hour, missing my family, the smell of chocolate wafted across the narrow Zürichsee from the Lindt chocolate factory directly opposite. And in a tenebrous time, sweet dark powder turned elixir and stimulant, bridging the conflicting effects of that hour.

In his work, Jung, like theologian Paul Tillich[2] and philosopher Philip Wheelwright,[3] observed how symbols bridge opposites, and do so by honoring the claim of two entities that otherwise might be at odds. When Robbie Burns writes that his love is like a red, red rose, we do not think he has fallen in love with a plant but rather that he has employed an image, the rose plant, as a rhetorical device. While the numinous powers of the Beloved are beyond comprehension and definition, one can approach the inexplicable by way of the more apprehensible beauty of the rose. If Burns had fallen for the plant, he would only have written a potpourri of signs: images that link one to the explicable and more knowable world of the vegetative. But his aim is higher; he wishes to bring us into the precincts of mystery. He does not say she is a rose, but that she is like a rose. This intimation brings us near the mystery but can only point in its direction; it can intimate only because she is beyond ordinary definition.

The evocation of the rose image, perhaps clichéd in our time, provides a bridge to the essential mystery. Both of those dogmatic entrepreneurs I described wish to dispel the mystery in service to the ego's uncertainty and anxiety generated by ambiguity. Generally speaking, the chief agenda of the ego is to protect the organism, see to its adaptation and survival. Understandable, even necessary, as that agenda is, it often operates in ways that finesse, deny, or manipulate the elusive mystery of things.

When one engages the numinosum, the essential encounter with mystery, it is wordless, imageless. That is the phenomenon. The epiphenomenon is the secondary process, the encapsulation by consciousness of the image that arises out of that felt encounter. So one might be inclined to say of Zeus, to choose one example from many, that his etymological root means "brightening" or "lightening." Thus we might say, "O, this is a sun god! Understandable . . . given how all life depends on the abiding presence of that gaseous ball in the sky." Now we have a concept the ego can accept, reject, or store away for a rainy day, but the syzygetic link to the mystery fades by the hour. Just as Eurydice fades when Orpheus turns and looks at her, so the numinosum slips away as the harsh sun rises to high noon.

But remember, Zeus is not a sun god per se. For the original encounters, "Zeus" embodied the wonder of "being brightened" or "being lightened"—that is to say, being suffused with light in a felt, moving fashion. To be suffused by this "light" is the religious experience: moving, wordless, transformative. Later come the systematizers, those who, with the best of intentions, create mythologies, theologies, and institutions to protect and transmit the numinosity of the original encounters. But, sadly, the numinosity wanes and disappears, leaving behind concepts and practices to defend against the "nonbelievers." And as soon as the schisms develop, true believers contend with each other for the title of the "true" true believer. And after true believers collide, one may expect the rack, the gallows, and the stake to be rolled out to the center of the village to expunge the heretics.

This devolution of the original power of numinosity into a concept, a practice, or dogmatic image leads to the oldest of religious sins: idolatry. One worships the image, already an artifact of ego consciousness that leads one further and further from the mystery. This almost inevitable fate of primal images leads us to the troubling conclusion that from time to time one must destroy one's image lest it devolve into something too familiar and devoid of energy. Iconoclasm is a form of religious fervor and respect, hence my invoking Baudelaire and Bukowski rather than "religious" poets like T. S. Eliot. Or as one widely disputed literary source put it, even for the best of writers, from time to time one has to "kill one's darlings."

It is natural for ego consciousness to be drawn to the image that arises out of the mystery, for the mystery itself remains shrouded in the invisible realm. Just as the traditional task of the religious has been to track the movement of the invisible realm as it enters and shapes the cerements of the visible realm, so it is analogously the task of the analyst today. However, the image's capacity to link one to the numinosum erodes over time, and especially through repetition. The degradation of this linking effect leads subsequent generations to focus on the image itself rather than on that to which it once pointed. This inevitably leads to idolatry. The more we institutionalize this image, the further we get from its energizing source.

Imagine Southern Zeus State University, Zeus T-shirts, Zeus drinking mugs, Zeus catechisms. Some of these phenomena rise out of an honest desire to recover the felt experience of the aboriginal suffusion by the mystery, and some of these phenomena rise out of an honest desire to make a buck, or a drachma.

In 1977, I was sitting in a class in Zürich when I first heard that paragraph where Jung asks the question "Where did the gods go when they left Olympus?"[4] What a remarkable sentence!

And who would dare, or care, to ask it in the twentieth century? Of course, Jung's response is equally provocative. The gods left Olympus and entered the solar plexus of the modern. So we are to find the old gods in the fevers of the flesh, the disquietude of the stomach, the contentions of the heart, and so on. Those old energies that once took the provisional shape of gods persist and carry on their ancient battles. Today, we call these agitations and skirmishes complexes, neuroses, somatoform diseases, personality disorders, and the like. The once godly realm is now a contentious landscape, a mélange of psychoneurotic diseases. As those primal energies are neglected, medicated, or projected, they pathologize and configure a broken terrain traversed by pharmacology and psychotherapy.

Once that primal link is severed or eroded, pandemonium erupts and all demons appear—addictions; getting high by any means; compelling ideologies; intrapsychic conflicts tragically projected and transferred to one's neighbors; and the war goes on. Never ask anyone of what they are unconscious or most afraid. They won't thank you for the hint and will begin to think you are the cause of their problem.

So rich are the heuristic possibilities of that paragraph that I determined that such would be my thesis at the C. G. Jung-Institut, and later, the book of the same title, *Tracking the Gods: The Place of Myth in Modern Life*. While it is perhaps the most important book I ever wrote, it is among the least read, as "myth" is already a disqualifier for the attention of the modern reader, for who has any interest in the gods anymore? But I have never forgotten that paragraph, nor the referred task it brought to my soul in this land and culture so distant from the first sunrise when Zeus rose over the mountain range and illumined the tossing Aegean.

When our ancestors felt the slippage of the numinous, they raised the ante considerably. Rather than just leave cornmeal and drink to appease the coy gods, why not the corn-maiden herself, her heart just pulled from her anxious chest? Her sundered body becomes the sacrifice, the thing rendered sacred by the solemnity of the services and the aspirant hearts of the pilgrims who stood before the stone altar. As the French polymath, historian, literary critic, and philosopher René Girard noted, the ritualization of violence slays the violence of the heart, and its propitiation abides for a season, perhaps until the next round is required. Inevitably, the urgent and inquiring heart must escalate its efforts, and hence the fervor and fever of fanaticism.

While the spirit of modernity—beginning perhaps with Shakespeare in the West and our brother Hamlet serving as the first modern acutely aware of his inner division as the source of the disorder—begins to pull at the loose threads of the fabric that knits a culture together, in time the strands unravel and the protective garment falls to the earth and is trodden underfoot. And then one walks nakedly into the land of Beckett's Vladimir and Estragon and sits amid the waste for some guy named Godot who apparently is running behind schedule. And thus, our vacant time is mostly filled by someone humming "By the rivers of Babylon, there we sat down, and yea we wept when we remembered Zion," or by a mad rush to purchase something . . . anything.

But the busy, anxious mind of those who wait never ceases. The anxious mind fills the empty spaces with many phantasies, each carrying the invisible imprint of its projective origins. We do not plan projections; they happen, perhaps triggered by external events, perhaps catalyzed by inner tensions. And so our subjective contents and framing categories leave us and enter the world to light upon objects, ideas, even people. When this archaic energy is exhausted, it withdraws and gods die, the numinous goes underground again, and one even may fall out of love. Students of culture, mythologists, and anthropologists can examine the lingering patterns those projections instituted and work backward to form a revealing Rorschach of the psyche at a particular time or place or person.

We have been amply warned by Søren Kierkegaard that the god that can be named is not God and by Paul Tillich that god is the god who appears from behind the god who just disappeared. To lose one's link to that numinosum is to be in grave peril, subject to the loudest, shrillest noisemaker or the seductive voice that tells us what we most want to hear. In short, our theologies, our institutions, inevitably reveal more about us than about the elusive gods.

In that 1912 book, *Symbols of Transformation*, Jung describes how our psyches operate autonomously to forage about and settle on images that, for the moment, may serve as the bridge to the numinous. Those images, for a while, serve as symbols; namely, transformers that convert libido from the instinctual realm to the spiritual realm. The spiritual realm is not to be prized more than the instinctual, for, as Jung noted repeatedly, separation from the instinctual creates most of our disorders and generates ephemera in our heads that cause lethal mischief among the nations. When one is gripped by an archetypal image, one is lifted out of the space-time continuum into the timeless zone of the Immortals. But one cannot remain there. The gods, in their godly way, move on and leave our images and institutions for the dustbin of history. The "lightening" that occurred when the symbol was doing its pontific work brings one the energy of the numinous. When that energy departs, a crisis of meaning occurs, whether acknowledged consciously or not. It is in those darker, sterile hours that harm is frequently done to self and others. And, frequently, those institutions left behind lose sight of their mission to occasion primal experience of the numinous with practices and substitute self-perpetuation, self-congratulation, and stern adherence to dogma, in preserving the institution itself.

All the while, the gods are not really absent; they are simply elsewhere, perhaps for a millennium or two. And those left behind are no longer participants in a sacred drama, but traverse a secular landscape filled with tempting blandishments but little that feeds the hungering spirit. The failure of well-intended institutions and practices to illumine and personalize the presence of the godly energies is why the light has gone out for so many. It is not enough to preserve the images that once rose from the archetypal encounter; their forgotten task is to channel developmental libido via personal experience and stir the heart as well as persuade the brain.

The etymology of the word "religion" derives from two Latin words, one "to bind back to" (*religare*) and the other "to take into careful account" (*religere*). The former is a tacit confession of loss, estrangement, and desire for reconnection. The second illustrates the seriousness and magnitude of the invitation to sup with the transcendent Other. That the numinosum may at any moment depart, leaving but a husk behind, is a constant reminder that the human soul is the arena but not the cause of the transit of the gods. I once had an analysand who dreamt that Divinity was the energy that suffused the tungsten alloy in a lightbulb and rendered it luminous. But the numinosity was the energy, not the lightbulb. No one collects lightbulbs after the energy has departed, but they will hang on to the theologies and cultural forms of their ancestors, seeking to reanimate the light through rigid practices that may imitate but never really illuminate.

So, extending this application to analytic psychology, Jungians sometimes refer in their baffling way to a neurosis as "a neglected god." What they mean by this locution is that the energy, once mediated through the archetypal agency, has departed, and the individual's efforts to regenerate something—which was never within their power in the first place—proves futile. It is at this moment that the tenuous hold of ego slips and falls into a crisis of meaning, occasioning determined efforts at revival of the primal encounter. When such regenerative efforts fail, as they must, the person falls into the grip of the neurosis, namely, a splitting from one's own receptive depths and a conversion to the frenetic world of symptomatology. Taking the symptom seriously does not then mean more medication; it means that one has to trace its threads back into the depths where the mystery lies waiting and whence a new incarnation of mystery may emerge.

It is because of our insidious displacement of the depth, and the resonant and responsive dynamics of our own souls, that thoughtful spirits such as Jung had to "invent" depth psychology to explore the turned-in-upon-themselves souls of patients. We may not use the word "gods" to describe the affect-laden, highly charged images that arise in our troubled dreams, but we are once again obliged to bear witness to such images that do arise from the depths of the individual. It is not the group that will illumine the individual; it is the individual who may share the encounter with the numinous with the group. As the greatest task of the second half of life is the recovery of personal authority in the face of group allegiance, so the individual soul is the smithy through which the gods reenact their ancient dance.

In sum, we have seen that time is the enemy of any hope of retaining the numinous image. Once the energy has expressed itself, it leaves a husk behind. The worship of that husk is idolatry, serving perhaps the immediate need of the ego but driving the numinous further away. The suffering of this loss of linkage to the numinous is what has made depth psychology necessary as a vehicle for a new approach to the precincts of the numinous. In his memoir *Memories, Dreams, Reflections*, Jung wrote,

The need for mythic statements is satisfied when we frame a view of the world which adequately explains the meaning of human existence in the cosmos, a view which springs from our psychic wholeness, from the cooperation between the conscious and the unconscious. Meaninglessness inhibits the fullness of life and is therefore equivalent to illness. Meaning makes a great many things endurable—perhaps everything. No science will ever replace myth, and a myth cannot be made out of any science. For it is not that "God" is a myth but that myth is the revelation of a divine life in man.[5]

Our urgent hearts cannot create the new myth, but the soul will surely be the place in which it first makes its appearance. This summons to look within, wait with patience, and open to the entreaty of the mystery is why I cited the dissolute Charles Bukowski as a "saintly" exemplar. He didn't understand his father, nor the violence, but he did intuit that his father could not "understand what was attacking him from within." So even the child knew what the father could only suffer—and thereby bring suffering to others—that the cause and cure of the soul's malaise could be solved not by violence, or a new and shiny object, or power or wealth or status, but by a quiet waiting for whatever within wished to make its appearance known. So it is for the rest of us to wait, to attend (these verbs are the etymology of the word "therapeuein," from which we get "therapy"). The open mind, the receptive spirit, the inquiring soul are venues in which the gods will again make their presence known, for a while, before departing in their inexplicable way.

The gods, it seems, have no imperative to make sense to us or deliver their itinerary to us in advance. We trace their foaming passage on the spindrift of history long after they have already left for their next port of call. That is why they are "the gods," and we are not.

Epilogue

Remembering Jung's warning that we cannot take a person any further than we have traveled ourselves, I find myself still curious, still amazed at the simplest of things, and still wanting to know what is going on beneath the surface. As a result of this inquiry, life never ceases to be heuristic, never loses its capacity to challenge the assumptions that carried us through yesterday but prove insufficient for today. As a partner, as a citizen, and as an analyst, I have to keep asking these questions of myself lest I be caught in the old, old narratives that exist within. And so must you, dear reader. Keep asking the large questions. Large questions give you a larger life. Large questions restore to you the sovereignty of your soul. Adaptations, necessary as they once were, blur and blunt this need to keep heuristic questions before you. Understandably, the needs for peace, for satiety, for safety, press all about us. But when these needs take over, we wind up with diminished lives.

For each of us, the turn of the wheel of time brings us over and over to the question "How shall you live in the face of this situation over which you, seemingly, have no control?"

Jung's most popular observation is that most of our problems stem from being separated from our instincts. As our journey begins in utter powerlessness and dependency upon those whom fate has assigned to us, we survive as creatures of adaptation. Over time, repeated daily, these adaptations become reflexive, even autonomous responses to the challenges that arise from our families and our assigned culture. No wonder one grows a stranger to oneself. No wonder we become our own worst enemy. We even cling to our maladaptive behaviors, for they are the boat that brought us this far. Sometimes the natural maturation process allows us to outgrow our childhood fears and concomitant behaviors, but many times they become institutionalized within us as shadow governments. Often it takes a crisis, a loss of energy, or a set of troubling consequences that oblige us to stop and finally take account, perhaps start therapy, or perhaps tough it out on our own.

We can see why the recovery of personal authority becomes the signal project of the second half of life. Finding and separating the tangled threads of personal authority from the plethora of voices crying for our loyalty within takes on a newly felt urgency. This sorting and sifting project, this task of discernment, rises out of a newly found attitude of critical awareness. "Where is this coming from in me?" and "Have I been here before?" and "Does this path make me larger, or does it diminish my journey?" are the kinds of questions required of all of us to evolve into a more authentic presence.

Sooner or later each of us is obliged to traverse the savannahs of suffering. Sooner or later evil makes its way into our lives, along with loss, defeat, and the seductive temptations of lassitude and avoidance. But even the darkness is part of the richness of this journey we call our lives. No matter what happens to us from out there, so much more is asked of us from within. Sustaining the energy, the focus, the fierce commitment to growth and learning is difficult but critical to the depth and dignity of our journey. For each of us, the turn of the wheel of time brings us over and over to the question "How shall you live in the face of this situation over which you, seemingly, have no control?" This question personalizes the challenge to us directly.

In a letter Jung wrote to Olga Fröbe-Kapteyn in the 1950s, he said the opus of individuation consists of three parts, of which psychology can only help with the first stage: insight. Then, he said, come the moral qualities of the individual: courage to face whatever must be faced and persistence and endurance over time until one has lived into a different place.

I am also always reminded of Jung's query "What supports you when nothing supports you?" Sooner or later, the constructed edifice of the false self will erode, even collapse, and then one enters the dark night of the soul. Will we, in all that intimidating darkness, find even a scintilla of light that leads us through and out of the dark forest? If we find, hold on to, and risk that glimmer of light, then we know we carry something that transcends the ordinary ego limitations that bind us to the dreary cycle of repetition. Such a person knows from then on that she or he is never alone in their aloneness, that she or he is never bereft of guidance within, and that if we simply try to do the next right thing as we believe it to be right, something within will rise and support us.

In the vast star-flung ocean of the universe, the tiny human soul has a resilience and a buoyancy that one does not know . . . until one knows it. Remember how poet Emily Dickinson put it: "The Sailor cannot see the North—but knows the Needle can." Her insight reminds us that when we venture forth on the high seas of an uncertain voyage, we must remember to bring and trust the compass within that tells us the true north of the soul.

We must daily, but non-morbidly, recall Stanley Kunitz's reminder: "I only borrowed this dust." Sooner or later, we have to return the loan. I remain deeply grateful for the work of Carl Jung and other colleagues who have opened windows, methods, and larger perspectives along the way. They have sustained me, granted insight and hope, and told me I was not alone in my exile. Thus, when we come to the "return the dust" part, it helps to believe that we lived the rest of the journey with as much bien foi as we could manage.

Meanwhile, much of humanity cries out, "O where is the Beschert, the Beloved Other, where the magical elixir? O, where is the guru who will tell me what it is all about? Who will take care of me and allow me to avoid growing up and taking life on myself? Who will repair this broken world and make it all whole again?"

If one cannot link up to that Other, who would ever imagine that there was an Other within whose guiding presence has been quietly doing its work since our first moments out of the womb? Who would think that, most of all, we need to find what supports us when nothing supports us? Who would discover that we are never wholly alone, but that a goodly presence abides within, cares, and seeks an ongoing conversation with us? Alone, we are never wholly alone.

Only then may the celebration of life be truly lived. Life will break your heart, but at least then, you know you have a heart. Life will disappoint and fracture you, but it is also rich and nurturing and seeks to heal what is broken. As for me, here in my mid-eighties, I am flush with gratitude. While grieving the loss of so many loved ones, I am grateful for having them to love and for being loved by them in return. The future promises decline and death of the body, but for now, the spirit quickens and the boat waiting in the harbor has weighed anchor, for as Tennyson's "Ulysses" noted, "Death closes all: but something ere the end, / Some work of noble note, may yet be done, / Not unbecoming men that strove with Gods."[1]

As consolation for these losses and perturbations of the soul, and as gratitude for all the wonderful moments life still brings, I offer each of you, dear readers, this modest gift of my translation of a lovely poem by Rainer Maria Rilke titled "Abend," or "Evening."

> The evening slowly transforms its garments
> held awhile for it by the archaic line of trees;
> and the twin lands you watch separate,
> one falling, one heaven-travelling.
> And leave you not belonging entirely to either,
> and still not yet as dark or still as the silent houses,
> nor yet as eternally committed
> as the stars which rise each night,
> but leave you, unutterably to sort out
> your life, with its journeys and returns,
> so that sometimes contained, sometimes unlimited,
> it grows within you . . . sometimes stone, and sometimes star.

APPENDIX

Ballykil Bound

The moment that they heard Ellen's diagnosis, he knew he was a lost man. She died five months later. Pancreatic cancer is vicious, unsparing. After the brief service at the graveside, after the lugubrious legal forms, after drinking too much too many nights, after the dwindling calls from their friends, he sat in the dark, talked to her one more time, and wept one more time. In the morning, he booked a one-way flight on Aer Lingus to Shannon.

He let their friends know, and their two children, Silvie in Portsmouth and Sam in Chicago, and arranged for the utility bills to be paid by a neighbor. Across the Atlantic he heard the song "Hotel California" play over and over on the plane's Muzak. People all around him were snoring, but he perseverated on that one sentence, "You can check out any time you like, but you can never leave." The house of sorrow was his new residence.

The bus ride to Ballykil, a village of a few thousand along the Western coast, took him two hours. After checking in to the local hotel, the Harp and Staff, he fell into the bed and slept. He had picked the town out on a map, knowing nothing of it whatsoever other than that it was small, far from anything but the sea, and a person could get lost there. When he googled the name of the town, he found it rose from the

Celtic, meaning "a church settlement," no doubt tracking back to the arrival of the missionaries from France and Italy a thousand years earlier. The collision of those two cultures, Mediterranean and pagan, drove a deep wedge in the Irish soul that remains after all the layers of history piled on top of it all. That sounded about right to him.

For three days after he arrived in Ballykil it rained, profusely rained. Each day he ventured out to get some exercise and slosh through the mud and puddles. At night he read, history mostly, anything to distract his mind, and hoped that he would be able to sleep through the night without dreaming of Ellen. Every time he saw her, she was in those terrible last days, and he wished he could rid himself of that image and replace it with the many that were so much more pleasant. On the fourth day, he walked out again, and it was merely drizzling.

The first person he met said, "Lovely day, isn't it?"

"Of course," he replied ironically. When the third said much the same thing he realized that the villagers were sincere; it was lovely compared to the pounding rains that he had just witnessed.

While walking down Parnell Street he came across a life-sized crucifix with a Mary forlornly standing at the base of the cross. Behind was a list of eleven names of men who had left Ballykil and never returned. And the date: 1916. At first he thought the shrine referenced the Easter Rising, and he shuddered to think how many had died in that doomed venture. But then he remembered the push on the Somme and realized that is where the men were slaughtered on a much vaster scale, nearly sixty thousand casualties in the first twenty-four hours of the advance. A "plummet-bound race," Yeats described them.

That night, while sitting in the pub, The Plough and Stars, he noticed a cavity in the plaster radiating across the wall behind the small stage where sometimes buskers were allowed to play for tips.

"What happened there?" he asked the bartender.

"We were going to get it fixed, but the usuals who hang out here think it's great for tourists, so we keep it there. That, my friend, is a bullet hole that cracked the plaster."

"How did a gun go off in this place?"

"Well, that is where Benny McCrae's last laugh happened."

"Benny McCrae?"

"Yes, Benny was an old vaudevillian. Actually well known in his time. Played a lot of the big places in Galway, Dublin, and even London. He was in his eighties, and some were thinking, even saying, he was getting a bit bonkers, you know. So one night, near four years ago, he was telling this joke. It's one we all know around here. I don't think he knew one we hadn't heard. Three villages—Lusk, Rush, and Loughshinny—were too small to have a pipe band of their own, so they got the idea to band together and raise money for uniforms. So this bloke goes to the old widow Mahan.

"Afternoon, Ma'am. Might ya give some money for uniforms for the Lusk, Rush, and Loughshinny pipe bands?"

"Ehhhh?" she says.

He speaks louder. "Might ya give some money for the Lusk, Rusk, and Loughshinny pipe band uniforms?"

"Ehhhh?"

Now he's yellin' at 'er. "Ya got any money for the Lusk, Rush, Loughshinny band?!"

"Ehhhh?"

So he's disgusted now, stomps off, and at the gate to her property he turns and says, "Fook you, ole lady!"

And Mrs. Mahan yells after him, "And fook you, and fook yer Lusk, Rush, Loughshinny band!"

"Well, no one laughed except Micky Reardon, who, frankly, would laugh at a funeral."

"I think it's funny."

"Well, Benny reaches in and says to the people sitting there with their Guinness, 'And fook you all too!' And then he pulled out a pistol and shot himself in the temple. That was his swan song, I guess, his last best joke."

"Holy shit . . . what a shock."

"Well, yes it was, and it covered that wall with blood and brains. Naturally I washed all that stuff off before the next day, but didn't get around to calling a plasterer for a while. By then, folks thought it should be left there for the tourists to ask about. As you just did."

"I am not a tourist."

"Well . . . what are you then? You don't live here permanently. What are you if you ain't a tourist?"

"I don't know," he said. "Perhaps a resident alien. . . ."

***

He spent a lot of time walking the littoral, occasionally climbing the hills that rose up sharply from the shingle. Up close the grey-green surf churned and flung out flecks of foam, and the sea creatures slipped back into the sand or the retreating waves. In the distant harbor, he saw boats lying sideways that only hours before had been upright, buoyant, and rocking side to side. Amazing that there could be such a tidal shift in such a short time. He never tired of watching it. And sometimes in the spindrift spume he saw a way to go forward and, in the next wave, an erasure as sure as the neap tide coming.

When he reached the crest of the cliff behind the beach and looked down, the lines of surf seemed regular, marching in rank order, even as they chaotically broke and crashed when he was level with them. *Order in chaos, chaos in order,* he thought, *been this way from the beginning.* Born inland, far inland amid corn fields and grain silos, he grew up longing to see the sea. When he first saw Lake Michigan as a child, he knew it must be the ocean because he couldn't see across the horizon to another shore, and when windy, he saw whitecaps—proof definitive he had seen the ocean.

Three weeks after arriving, standing at the tide's retreating edge, he looked up on the ridgeline and saw a group of figures standing at the top, silhouetted by the sinking sun. Two rode horses and the rest walked and carried staves or spears. Motionless, they looked down at him, and then toward the horizon as if scanning the scudding mist to see sails heading their way. Transfixed, he watched them for minutes, wondering what they were doing there, and then they turned and walked back over the edge of the hill and disappeared. The last visible, one of the horsemen, raised his staff or spear and seemed to gesture toward him. He raised his arm in return salute, but they had gone.

That night at The Plough and Stars, after the bangers, salad, and Harp beer, he sidled up to the bar.

"Mac?"

"Yes?"

"Let me tell you what I saw, or think I saw last evening, just before the sun went down." He spoke quickly but beneath his breath.

"Holy Mother of God! You saw them?"

"What did I see?"

"I can't tell you, really, nor can anyone else. Some folks have seen them, told 'bout them for centuries. We never tell strangers or the place would be crawling with tourists. Look what they did with Nessie in Scotland."

"But what the hell was it?"

"I don't know. The priests have told us for generations it's the Devil and his minions come to get your soul. It's good for keeping children in line. And half of us almost believe that. What else is there to think?"

"But, c'mon, you know better than that, Mac. What the hell?"

"Well, seems the only other alternative is to think there is a set of spirits of some kind from one of the old Celt days standing watch for invasions from the North. Even before the Vikings came through here, the Northmen used to raid the coastal villages. Folks here were terrified, and through the years the Northmen became like boogey men, or something like that."

"But what did I see?"

"I don't know. We don't know. But it is weird that you, an outsider, saw them. It's mostly been the locals through the years."

"Well, are they hostile?"

"Who knows. They ride up to the ridgeline, watch below, make gestures, and then pull back into the gathering night. But you have seen something, that is for sure."

"I couldn't be dreaming this, or hallucinating, if I saw what others have seen."

"No, I don't imagine you were."

After that conversation he didn't know whether to go back to the same place and watch for them or not. After a week, he went and nothing . . . nothing. He went every night and nothing. He began to question his own sanity then. *Did I really see something?* The silence was his answer.

***

As the September trees began to turn, he drove northward to Sligo, and then up to Drumcliffe Cemetery, where Yeats is buried. Over the grave, if you stood with your back to the old church, you could see the massif Ben Bulben. On the tombstone were Yeats's lines: "Cast a cold eye / On life, on death. / Horseman, pass by!"

Anyone who read Yeats knows those last lines were phony, sheer bravado. Few have written more passionately about their attachment to life, their resistance to death, and their commitment to continuing after this life. No cold eye on life here, but . . . allow the man to have his final say.

On the ground, inscribed in granite, is his better last testament:

> But I, being poor, have only my dreams;
> I have spread my dreams under your feet;
> Tread softly because you tread on my dreams.

That's more like it. Soft, open, anguished—that is the poet, not a cold eye at all.

So, standing before the grave of his favorite poet, he mused, "And what would be my epitaph, if I left one? What would I want to say? How might I want to be remembered?"

His placement of Ellen's ashes at the local columbarium was fresh to mind. All there was room for were their names and dates, so the question was moot. But still . . . it made him think on the matter.

He walked out of the cemetery, toward the great slope overlooking the valley, and stared at the summit. What came up for him finally was something simple but truthful: "Up to the end, he kept trying to figure it all out."

***

In October he woke one morning and had his same porridge the landlady had fixed for centuries, or so it seemed. Cold milk on top with a half cup of raisins, bread, and coffee. As good a meal to begin every day as someone could want.

He walked down into the village, light mist as always, and stopped at the newsstand to buy a copy of *The Irish Times*. The *International Herald Tribune* would never show in a small town like this. He stepped into a coffee shop and read the paper slowly, mostly looking for some US news, even some delayed scores of the football games. Mostly, it was Irish football and rugby, as one would expect in Ireland. Still, it was always frustrating not to have a hint of home. He had told the kids not to worry about him if he was out of touch for a while. He was just sorting things through, he said. When he finished the paper, he left it on the table for someone else, stepped onto the street, and headed toward the sea once more.

After a couple of blocks, he saw a lit window at Flaherty's Jewelry. Something to do. Then he saw it, a small emerald on a gold chain. Emeralds were Ellen's birth stone. May 11. He walked in and paid a little over two hundred Euros for the necklace and walked out toward the turbulent sea once more.

As he neared the dunes, he stopped, half-smiling, thinking of her surprise, and then said, "She's dead." Of course she's dead, has been all along. He stood in the mist, looking out toward the tossing sea. He turned. About that time, Mrs. Craig and her five-year-old were hurrying to school, having been delayed once more by the failure of the clock to wake them.

He walked to them and said, "Hello. What is your name, young lady?"

"Jenny."

"How old are you, Jenny?"

"Five. But I am almost six now . . . next month."

"Here is a birthday gift for a beautiful young lady, Jenny. Open it next month at home."

He walked away from them both before they could look inside the package. Ellen was dead. He knew it now.

***

One day, nearing six months after he arrived, he sat up in bed and said to himself, "It's time to go home. Time to get off my ass and go back to my work." After the morning porridge and coffee, he called Aer Lingus and booked his flight back three days from then, a window seat away from the sun, 18K on the Airbus 330-300. The night before leaving, he walked to the water's edge, stepping over the scattered sedge on the beach, stepping into the cold surf, and walked out farther than he had ever walked before. The next morning the Airbus left Shannon bound for Boston with seat 18K empty. Aileen Monroe was happy the seat was empty, for she could stretch out all the way home.

Notes

Chapter 1: Happiness: Find What You Love and Let It Kill You

1. Jack Gilbert, "A Brief for the Defense," Poetry Society of America, poetrysociety.org/poems/a-brief-for-the-defense.
2. Gustave Flaubert, "Letter to Louise Colet, 13 August 1846," Oxford Essential Quotations, 5th Online Edition, oxfordreference.com/display/10.1093/acref /9780191843730.001.0001/q-oro-ed5-00004457.
3. Microsoft Bing, "Funny Baby Pictures," bit.ly/3IhJfvQ.
4. Fleur Adcock, "Things," Scottish Poetry Library, scottishpoetrylibrary.org.uk/poem/things/.
5. Dr. Laurie Santos, "The Science of Well-Being Course by Yale University," Coursera, coursera.org/learn /the-science-of-well-being.
6. LibQuotes, "Nikos Kazantzakis Quote," libquotes.com /nikos-kazantzakis/quote/lba5k8n.

Chapter 2: Meta: Beyond, After, Across, Before

1. The Association Experiment involves reading a series of stimulus words and observing which ones evoke a "disturbance of consciousness," suggesting that something in the unconscious of the subject has been activated.
2. *The Nightmare*, Wikipedia, last modified May 2, 2024, en.wikipedia.org/wiki/The_Nightmare.

Chapter 3: Filling Our House with Gold: Unbidden Ideas and Compelling Behaviors

1. Marion Woodman, *Addiction to Perfection: The Still Unravished Bride* (Toronto: Inner City Books, 1982), 12.

Chapter 4: Active Imagination and the Encounter with the Daimon Within

1. William Butler Yeats, "Byzantium," Poetry Foundation, poetryfoundation.org/poems/43296/Byzantium.
2. Goodreads, "Paul Éluard Quote," goodreads.com/quotes /1045320-there-is-another-world-but-it-is-in-this-one.
3. Rainer Maria Rilke, "Archaic Torso of Apollo," Academy of American Poets, poets.org/poem/archaic-torso-apollo.

Chapter 6: Divided Soul/Divided Nation: Reflections on the American Electorate

1. Quote.org, "Louis Pasteur Quotes," quote.org/quote /one-does-not-ask-of-one-who-629537.
2. The Socratic Method, "Joseph de Maistre: Every country has the government it deserves," socratic-method.com /quote-meanings-french/joseph-de-maistre-every-country -has-the-government-it-deserves.
3. H. L. Mencken, "Bayard vs. Lionheart," *The Baltimore Evening Sun*, July 26, 1920.
4. C. G. Jung, *Collected Works of C. G. Jung, Volume 11: Psychology and Religion: West and East*, ed. and trans. Gerhard Adler and R. F. C. Hull (Princeton: Princeton University Press, 1970), 170.
5. C. G. Jung, *C. G. Jung Letters: Volume 2: 1951–1961*, eds. Gerhard Adler and Aniela Jaffé, trans. R. F. C. Hull (London: Routledge, 2015), 384.

6. C. G. Jung, "Wotan," in *The Collected Works of C. G. Jung, Volume 10: Civilization in Transition*, ed. and trans. Gerhard Adler and R. F. C. Hull (Princeton: Princeton University Press, 1970), 191.

7. Jung, *The Collected Works of C. G. Jung, Volume 10: Civilization in Transition*, 191.

8. One of the amazing qualities of sociopaths and narcissists is their talent for "spinning" events to justify and legitimize their behaviors and blame others. Normal "neurotic" people spin in their juices and feel bad, but the others quickly slip out of the noose of accountability and blame others.

9. H. L. Mencken, "Bayard vs. Lionheart," *The Baltimore Evening Sun*, July 26, 1920.

10. Emily Dickinson, "Letters from Dickinson to Higginson, 7 June 1862 (Letter 265)," Dickinson Electronic Archives, emilydickinson.org.

Chapter 7: When You Stare into the Abyss

1. Quote Investigator, "Don't Look Back. Something Might Be Gaining On You," quoteinvestigator.com/2020/11/02/gaining/.

Chapter 8: *Die Traumdeutung der Trauma*: The Meaning of Trauma

1. Ezra Pound, "Hugh Selwyn Mauberly [excerpt]," Academy of American Poets, poets.org/poem/hugh-selwyn-mauberly-excerpt.

2. William Shakespeare, *Macbeth*, (New York: Modern Library, 2009), 2.2.67.

3. Samuel Beckett, *Nohow On: Company, Ill Seen Ill Said, Worstward Ho* (New York: Grove Press, 1996), 89.

Chapter 9: Dark Divinity: The Problem of Evil, the Problem of Good

1. Goodreads, "John Steinbeck Quote," goodreads.com /quotes/220402-there-ain-t-no-sin-and-there-ain-t-no -virtue-there-s.
2. C. G. Jung, *C. G. Jung Letters, Volume 2: 1951–1961*, ed. and trans. Gerhard Adler and R. F. C. Hull (Princeton: Princeton University Press, 1961), 384.

Chapter 10: Bundles of Darkness/ Moments of Meeting: The Despoiled and Present State of the Soul

1. C. G. Jung, *Collected Works of C. G. Jung, Volume 5: Symbols of Transformation*, ed. and trans. Gerhard Adler and R. F. C. Hull (Princeton: Princeton University Press, 1977), 472.
2. Paul Tillich, *Theology of Culture* (Oxford: Oxford University Press, 1957).
3. Philip Wheelwright, *The Burning Fountain* (Bloomington, IN: Indiana University Press, 1954).
4. C. G. Jung, "Introduction to the Secret of the Golden Flower," in the *Collected Works of C. G. Jung, Volume 13: Alchemical Studies*, ed. and trans. Gerhard Adler and R. F. C. Hull (Princeton: Princeton University Press, 1968), 37.
5. C. G. Jung, *Memories, Dreams, Reflections*, ed. Aniela Jaffé, trans. Clara Winston and Richard Winston (New York: Pantheon, 1961), 340.

Epilogue

1. Alfred Tennyson, "Ulysses," Poetry Foundation, poetryfoundation.org/poems/45392/ulysses.

Bibliography

Arendt, Hannah. *Eichmann in Jerusalem: A Report on the Banality of Evil*. New York: Penguin, 2006.

Becker, Ernest. *The Denial of Death*. New York: Free Press, 1997.

Camus, Albert. *The Fall*. New York: Vintage, 1991.

———. *Resistance, Rebellion, and Death: Essays*. New York: Vintage, 1995.

Conrad, Joseph. *The Heart of Darkness*. New York: Everyman's Library, 1996.

Dostoevsky, Fyodor. *Notes from Underground*. New York: Penguin, 1992.

Goethe, Johann von. *Faust*. New York: Anchor, 1962.

Hollis, James. *The Broken Mirror: Refracted Images of Ourselves*. Asheville, NC: Chiron Books, 2022.

———. *Creating a Life: Finding Your Individual Path*. Toronto: Inner City Books, 2002.

———. *Finding Meaning in the Second Half of Life: How to Really Grow Up*. New York: Avery/Penguin, 2006.

———. *Swamplands of the Soul*. Toronto: Inner City Books, 1996.

Jung, C. G. *The Collected Works of C. G. Jung, Volumes 1–20*. Edited by Herbert Read, Michael Fordham, Gerhard Adler, and William McGuire. Translated by Gerhard Adler and R. F. C. Hull. Princeton: Princeton University Press, 1953–1979.

————. *C. G. Jung Letters: Volume 2, 1951–1961.* Edited by Gerhard Adler and Aniela Jaffé. Translated by R. F. C. Hull. London: Routledge, 2015.

————. *Memories, Dreams, Reflections.* Edited by Aniela Jaffé. Translated by Clara Winston and Richard Winston. New York: Pantheon Books, 1961.

MacLeish, Archibald. *J.B.: A Play in Verse.* New York: Houghton Mifflin, 1989.

Vaihinger, Hans. *The Philosophy of the "As If."* London: Routledge, 2021.

Van der Kolk, Bessel. *The Body Keeps the Score: Brain, Mind, and Body in the Healing of Trauma.* New York: Penguin, 2015.

Woodman, Marion. *Addiction to Perfection: The Still Unravished Bride.* Toronto: Inner City Books, 1982.

Yalom, Irving. *Staring at the Sun: Overcoming the Terror of Death.* New York: Jossey-Bass, 2009.

About the Author

James Hollis, PhD, is a licensed Jungian analyst in private practice in Washington, DC. Originally from Springfield, Illinois, he graduated from Manchester University in 1962 and Drew University in 1967. He taught humanities for 26 years in various colleges and universities before retraining as a Jungian analyst at the Jung Institute of Zurich, Switzerland (1977–82). He served as executive director of the Jung Educational Center in Houston, Texas, for many years. He was executive director of the Jung Society of Washington until 2019, and now serves on its board of directors. He is a retired senior training analyst for the Inter-Regional Society of Jungian Analysts, was first director of training of the Philadelphia Jung Institute, and is vice-president emeritus of the Philemon Foundation. Additionally, he was a professor of Jungian Studies for Saybrook University of San Francisco.

He has written twenty books, available in translations around the world, including *Living Between Worlds*, *What Matters Most*, and *Living an Examined Life*. He lives with his wife, Jill, an artist and retired therapist, near Washington, DC. Together they have three living children and eight grandchildren. For more, visit jameshollis.net.

About Sounds True

Sounds True was founded in 1985 by Tami Simon with a clear mission: to disseminate spiritual wisdom. Since starting out as a project with one woman and her tape recorder, we have grown into a multimedia publishing company with a catalog of more than 3,000 titles by some of the leading teachers and visionaries of our time, and an ever-expanding family of beloved customers from across the world.

In more than three decades of evolution, Sounds True has maintained our focus on our overriding purpose and mission: to wake up the world. We offer books, audio programs, online learning experiences, and in-person events to support your personal growth and awakening, and to unlock our greatest human capacities to love and serve.

At SoundsTrue.com you'll find a wealth of resources to enrich your journey, including our weekly *Insights at the Edge* podcast, free downloads, and information about our nonprofit Sounds True Foundation, where we strive to remove financial barriers to the materials we publish through scholarships and donations worldwide.

To learn more, please visit SoundsTrue.com/freegifts or call us toll-free at 800.333.9185.

Together, we can wake up the world.